RUG MONEY

How a Group of Maya Women Changed Their Lives through Art and Innovation

MARY ANNE WISE and CHERYL CONWAY-DALY

To Rod & Lori,
Thank you for being part of the rug hooking story. We are grateful for your friendship and support. — Cheryl

Thank you — amazing journey since the 1st encounter in the shop.... Mary Anne Wise

Thanks for all your support & friendship
Jody Slocum

10/3/18

Publisher: Linda Ligon
Associate Publisher/Editor: Karen Brock
Design: Anne Clark

Text © 2018 Mary Anne Wise and Cheryl Conway-Daly
Photography, except as noted © 2018 Joe Coca

Cover image: Members of the Chirijquiac rug-hooking group
Photo by Reyna Pretzantzin
Interior cover: Hooked rug by Micaela Churunel

THRUMS
BOOKS

306 North Washington Avenue
Loveland, Colorado 80537
USA

Printed in China by Asia Pacific Offset
Library of Congress Control Number: 2018931448

Dedication

To the women of Multicolores whose stories of courage and determination are told in the hope that they inspire others to action.

Acknowledgments

Early on, Reyna, Cheryl, Jody, and I saw the economic promise of the women's hooked rugs—a rare and fine thing in craft development work. Working as a Team, we dedicated ourselves to this promise. The scope of our work quickly became larger than any of us envisioned. To accomplish what followed, we enlisted help from legions of friends, colleagues, tour alumni, and others living in Guatemala, Canada, and the U.S. These folks held fundraisers, hosted hook-ins, lent their professionalism, offered counsel, put us up for a night or two, donated money and miles, materials, equipment, and much, much more. We are deeply grateful.

I acknowledge the role played by our skeptics. You caused us to reexamine our vision and as a result we sharpened our focus and toughened our resolve. You helped us become stronger.

I am grateful to the U.S.-based nonprofits who offered support at key junctures: Farmer to Farmer, The Maya Educational Foundation, and Sharing The Dream.

I am grateful to Jody Slocum whose indefatigable can-do attitude benefited the project from day one. Her friendship and constancy are a gift.

I'm grateful to my artist-husband Arne Nyen who saw the power and the promise hidden in the women's first rugs. His admiration for their artistry and his conviction that they were "on to something" fueled me forward. His advice and encouragement benefited the project, and me, along the way. That he tolerates my long absences is appreciated—it's not what he signed up for.

I'm grateful to Carmen Maldonado, "Carmencita," who made me a better teacher.

I'm grateful for Reyna Pretzantzin's honesty, friendship, vision, and guidance.

I'm inspired by my co-author, Cheryl Conway and her staggering sense of commitment to this project: without her dedication, the project would have withered away.

Thank you for the feedback given by my readers Ann Fox and Burnie Bridge. A special thank you to my reader, poet John Graber, for his generosity.

I'm amazed by photographer Joe Coca's ability to shed his corporeal body and then insert himself into the shoot without anyone noticing his presence. Impressive.

Thank you Karen Brock for the heart and clarity you brought to this book. You asked the right questions.

Thank you Mary Littrell for your early interest in this project—your attention felt validating to all of us.

Thank you Linda Ligon. You said the words that convinced me to write this book, and then you gave me the opportunity to do so.

They say "to teach is to learn," and in working with the women of Multicolores, I discovered things in myself I didn't know I possessed. I am forever grateful for this learning opportunity.

—Mary Anne

It is one of the great honors of my life to work with Reyna, Mary Anne, and Jody. Their commitment, hard work, vision, and compassion inspire me to keep reaching further. I have huge admiration and respect for each of them.

It has been a pleasure to collaborate with Mary Anne on this book. She is a gifted writer and has truly written from the heart, bringing the women's stories to life in a tender and compelling way. Mary Anne is tireless in her support of Multicolores and the Maya women rug hookers. She is their teacher, their champion, their friend.

I am grateful to Reyna for being my friend. We have worked side by side as equals, always united in purpose, and together we have achieved some remarkable things. Reyna passionately believes in the skills and resourcefulness of her Maya people. She is a talented leader, mentor, and facilitator, always envisioning Multicolores's next step.

I appreciate Jody for her energy and cheerfulness. During those, "that wasn't supposed to happen" moments, she is first on the phone to sort things out. She just gets things done. Her love of Guatemala and the Maya people is evident on the many tours we have led together. Jody is driven by a sense of justice and a very good heart.

I am so proud of the Multicolores rug hookers. Their artistry astounds me, their courage to persevere and to learn rug hooking, overcoming many obstacles in pursuit of a better life for themselves and their families, is humbling. We work as a team; if we stumble, we are there to pick each other up.

We have been fortunate to have the support of donors, tour alumni, fellow artists, nonprofit colleagues, and dear friends who have given their time, knowledge, expertise, and resources to support the work of Multicolores. They have been cheering the women on every step of the way; quite simply, we couldn't do it without them.

Thank you to Linda Ligon and the Delta Foundation. You have been there from the very beginning, when the Rug-Hooking Project was just a whiff of an idea. Your constancy and support have allowed us to keep moving forward, offering more opportunities to disenfranchised women living in Guatemala.

Thank you to the Thrums Books team for their professionalism, patience, and unflappability. We enjoyed Karen and Joe's visit to Guatemala. Joe's beautifully captured photographs of the women and their rugs really bring this book to life. Karen, sensitive to the plights of the Maya women, was moved by their stories as we all are; we knew the crafting of this book would be safe in her hands.

Finally, thanks to my family in Northern Ireland and my friends for always encouraging me in my work. And to my husband Ryan for his love, understanding, and support. We met in Guatemala so I know he gets it, even though this means long absences away from home.

My mother is the strongest woman I know, so I knew growing up that we as women could do many things.

—Cheryl

- Quiejel
- Chichicastenango
- Totonicapán
- Chirijquiac
- Sololá
- Chuacruz
- Patanatic
- Panajachel
- Guatemala City
- Antigua

MEXICO

GUATEMALA

NORTH

Foreword

As the 2014 International Folk Art Market in Santa Fe, New Mexico, opened, customers jammed into a new market booth, its tables piled high with hooked rugs from Guatemala. Dressed in her vibrant *traje* (traditional clothing), rug artist Yolanda from the Multicolores artisan group watched in amazement. Customers reached for rugs, exclaiming, "I've never seen anything like this," "What bold, colorful designs," or "Each one is unique, so different." During the market weekend, Yolanda sold 250 rugs, ending with a near-empty booth. Based on final market tabulations, Multicolores ranked as one of the top three sellers—an astonishing achievement for a first-time market participant.

As I watched customers purchase rug after rug, I reflected beyond the buying frenzy to the remarkable evolution of rug hooking in a weaving culture. Five years earlier, Guatemalan weavers and embroiderers, desperate for income to support their families, struggled with stagnant sales in the saturated tourism market. The fair-trade organizations through which some women sold faced challenges in assisting with new product development. Now, just five years later, Yolanda and Multicolores participated with vibrant new textiles in one of the world's largest and most rigorously juried folk art markets.

This book chronicles the eight-year journey of Mary Anne Wise, an accomplished rug maker and designer from Wisconsin, the leadership team within Guatemala, and a group of motivated Guatemalan women who took on the challenge of learning a new textile skill. Along the way, the women emerged as talented artists creating one-of-a-kind rugs that spoke to their rich Maya aesthetic—rugs that captured the attention of international buyers. As I watched Yolanda and her customers in 2014, I realized that the Multicolores story had much to offer the larger international community focused on sustainable enterprise development.

The Multicolores rug project provides insight into the critical topic of folk art innovation, a subject ripe for discussion as artists seek new and sustainable ways to maintain their artistic traditions. Historically, folk art served functional and aesthetic needs of community members. Potters molded clay vessels for carrying water, carpenters carved wood boxes for storage, and weavers wove textiles for clothing. As cheaper, machine-produced alternatives replaced artisanal products, local demand for the handmade waned. Eager to sustain their traditions, artists approached the global market as an opportunity to maintain their culture and create products for contemporary use. Entering the international market demands challenging product innovation. Artisans must reach beyond their home communities to design for customers whose lifestyles are vastly different from their own.

The artists' focus on innovation comes at a time when customers are registering dissatisfaction with product standardization in the twenty-first-century marketplace. Instead, buyers seek products that exhibit uniqueness and creativity. Indrasen Vencatachellum, an expert in the culture and creative industry, has described, "At a time when everything is available everywhere, objects with a genuine local and cultural connection have true added value for consumers and seem well placed for growth."

As a foreword to *Rug Money–How a Group of Maya Women Changed Their Lives through Art and Innovation*, I offer a series of themes that provide context for considering the strong path that Multicolores charted in folk art innovation. These themes are drawn from my twenty-five years of working with artisan groups in Central America, West Africa, and Central, South, and East Asia. The issues highlight challenges artisan groups face as they pursue a path toward innovation. They illustrate strategies that have worked and pitfalls confronted in design and marketing. Themes relevant to the rug-hooking project include approaches for product innovation, education for artisans with limited formal education, control of design as cultural property, leadership for sustainability, and quality-of-life impacts.

Together, these themes lay the groundwork for addressing the larger question: What can be learned from the rug-hooking project that other artisan groups can glean, modify, and apply as they work toward innovation for international markets?

Innovation within tradition

Textile folk art is deeply embedded in cultural and community traditions. Passed down within families and across generations, folk art encompasses two bodies of cultural property. Long-honed technologies and available materials guide *how* textiles are produced. Aesthetic norms for shape, motifs, color, and product guide *what* is produced. Both traditional technology and aesthetics offer avenues for change. Commonly, artisans integrate the two in tandem as they explore avenues for innovation within an artistic tradition. Other artists focus their innovation on aesthetic change only, while retaining their technology.

Mary Anne's experimental rug project took yet another approach to innovation. She added a completely new technology to Maya women's textile repertoire while preserving their aesthetic. In earlier trips to Guatemala, Mary Anne observed Maya women drawing from a reservoir of aesthetic knowledge when weaving their *huipil* (blouse) designs in a dazzling palette of reds, greens, blues, and yellows. Parameters for colors, motifs, and design placement differed from one village to the next. She also observed a plentiful supply of secondhand clothing shipped in bales from the United States and sold in retail shops. Ways to upcycle these inexpensive fabrics surfaced in Mary Anne's mind.

Mary Anne wondered if the weavers might be interested in this new approach and enjoy drawing from what they owned—the aesthetic of their prized huipil designs—to hook high-quality, one-of-a-kind rugs that she believed would sell in the international market. Would the women be able to transfer their Maya aesthetic from a weaving culture to the new skill of rug hooking?

Ventures in controlling cultural property— teaching artisans with little formal schooling

As artisans enter the global market, they commonly rely on outside designers to guide their market entry. Yet outsiders may have little knowledge of indigenous aesthetics. Often they are unaware of patterns of daily life for balancing artisanal activity with heavy loads of household work. External designers may introduce new aesthetics or technologies that hold little meaning for the artisans and cannot be sustained for further product development once the outsider departs. The designer, focused on new products for a specific design season, may not return once a design project is completed. The artisans are left with little understanding of or control over future design innovation from their traditional heritage.

To counteract this dependency on outside designers, educators are exploring new models for design education with indigenous artisans who have little to no formal schooling. These models, used in organizations around the world, foster transformation of weavers, dyers, and embroiderers from artisans dependent upon external designers to artists taking control of their design work in the global market. Graduates of these design programs may continue to work closely with outside designers. However, the balance of the interactions changes. The artists bring their new expertise in product innovation and firm expectations for collaboration to the conversation.

These education initiatives exhibit several common parameters. Students who are already skilled artisans devote several short periods of study at a school. Classes are spaced across six months to a year so artisans can integrate their schooling with the heavy demands of home and work. Factors contributing to the design school's success include offering artisans time away from their homes for focused exploration of their craft in new directions and assigning homework for trying out new ideas in small units of learning over the course of a year. The artisans learn to source innovative new visual concepts as inspired by local heritage and natural environment. Artisans who rarely speak up in public to express their ideas gain confidence to give and receive critique in the schools' safe environments.

The rug-hooking project built on these successes in providing a different example of education, in its case, to fit the Guatemalan context. Teachers and students collaborated in not only learning the techniques of high-quality rug hooking, but in developing novel ways to teach the transfer of design elements from traditional *huipils* to hooked rugs.

Mary Anne believed that for the project to become sustainable, she as an outside designer must no longer be essential to its operation. To accomplish this goal, the rug project needed to evolve beyond educating artisans as design innovators. Mary Anne assessed that if a curriculum could be developed to coach a small group of artists to become *design teachers*, more artisans could acquire sustainable income opportunities. Multicolores would no longer be dependent on Mary Anne's design direction. She could transition into the role of project advisor. Ensuing chapters tell of the innovative curriculum for teaching design criteria and for training teachers among a group of women who had rarely or never entered a formal classroom.

Proof of the successful transfer of knowledge to the design teachers became evident one day in late 2013. Mary Anne and Jody, who helped sell Multicolores's rugs in the United States, examined several shipments of new rugs. They admired the work of familiar artists from their classes, some of whom by now had developed recognizable individual styles. On this day, however, they were surprised to discover rugs affixed with tags bearing the names of women they had not taught nor met. For Mary Anne and Jody, the unfamiliar names signified that the project was working. The rug-hooking techniques, along with the design criteria, had been passed on to new rug hookers by the community-based teachers whom the Multicolores team had trained.

Organizational leadership

Leadership in artisan development projects requires a critical nucleus of expertise and experiences to succeed in the highly competitive market for handmade cultural products. At a minimum, these include artistic professionalism in product design and development, market knowledge of customer demand, deep understanding of artisans' lives in cultural context, and management expertise for uniting people, handling a complex product supply chain, and achieving fiscal stability.

All too often, one or more of these skills has been missing in artisan projects, as was evident in the early years of fair trade and other nongovernmental organization (NGO) projects. While early leaders exhibited deep commitment toward advancing artisan well-being, they often had minimal design or global marketing experience. For some leaders, their early resistance to guiding product design was equated with outsider intervention in local cultural patterns. Other groups lacked experience in establishing budgets for achieving strategic growth. A team with limited expertise across design and management capability is ill-suited for the new, competitive marketplace and encounters potentially disastrous consequences.

Multicolores's four-person leadership team was a fortuitous confluence of women whose leadership skills encompass crucial qualities of design, marketing, management, and cultural insider expertise. As is common in artisan development projects, the team of Mary Anne, Jody, Reyna, and Cheryl did not start with a well-designed strategic plan or template for how to proceed. Rather, the group creatively experimented in building the organization. Over time, their focus evolved and expanded—first with the women as rug hookers, then as artists and teachers, and now as household and community leaders. As the team experimented, their overarching vision to enhance artisans' income generation sustained their commitment to each other and to the rug-hooking artists.

The Multicolores team provides insights on the essential contribution of each team member's leadership skills to the project's success, answering key questions: From what artistic reservoir did Mary Anne draw in teaching rug design in new and novel ways? What cultural experiences guided Reyna, an indigenous Maya woman, in gently but firmly instructing the artisans in the rug-hooking classes and in follow-up production and quality control? What did the two on-the-ground leaders, Cheryl and Reyna, see in the project that kept them going, even when taking a pay cut or working for a period without pay?

How did Jody's logistic and problem-solving background help Multicolores survive and flourish during significant organizational junctures?

Quality of life

Robert Chambers, a longtime leader in international development policy, offers a model of well-being that applies in understanding impacts from artisan work. He calls for multiple indicators—economic, social, and psychological—in assessing quality of life. When women in artisan groups around the world are asked about how their lives have changed by earning income, they initially answer with observable outcomes. Examples of housing improvements, schooling for children, nutritional enhancements, and better health care prevail. Yet if pushed to identify a single most important difference, the women turn to highly personal and profound emotional stories. In coming together with other women in workshops, they learn that their problems are other women's problems as well. Through deep discussions and woman-to-woman encouragement, the women lose their fear of making decisions on their own. They acquire strength to speak up and become leaders for their families and communities.

For the women of Multicolores, by 2017 sales from rugs had far surpassed the women's previous earnings. Interviews with more than forty artists confirm socioeconomic changes in quality of life similar to those identified among other global artisans. Improvements in housing and water supplies along with greater consumption of protein frequent the Multicolores stories.

However, several changes are unique to the rug-hooking project—one related to marketing and the second to personal identity. It is rare that artisans get the opportunity to meet customers who live thousands of miles away. In contrast, several Multicolores rug hookers have had the opportunity to interact face-to-face with their international customers during sales events in the United States. Others have met and formed friendships with U.S. women who have traveled to Guatemala on rug-hooking tours. During these interactions, artisans learned that customers value individualism in their rug designs and are attracted to rugs that echo the dazzling motifs of traditional Guatemalan textiles. The artisans also heard that the upcycling of used clothes to rugs is a selling point for attracting sustainability-oriented customers. Through these interactions, the women gained valuable marketing expertise and encouragement for designing yet more saleable rugs.

In a second example, the project's unique focus on supporting women artisans to become rug-hooking artists distinguishes it from other projects. The women's narratives about becoming artists convey deep transformative change in perceptions of their personal human value and dignity. They began to view life and their role in it differently. These personal changes from artisan to artist offer important new documentation of the change that can come about when women have opportunities for sustainable income and a chance to develop their artistic talents.

Sixty new rug hookers and a look to the future

Looking back to 2009, Mary Anne arrived for her first rug-hooking classes with lesson plans in hand. She soon laid those plans aside as she quickly became convinced that how she taught before would change in Guatemala. As Mary Anne frequently says, "It *began* with getting one thing right, and letting that thing inform the next." After eight years, Multicolores looks to the future with both optimism and greater insight for addressing future challenges. The women's new identity as artists and women of strength nourishes Multicolores's evolving vision for its next stage—a women's leadership program. It seems appropriate to alter Mary Anne's earlier words, "It *continues* with getting one thing right, and letting that thing inform the next."

—*Mary Littrell, Santa Fe, 2017*

Hooked rug by Zoila Calgua.

Table of Contents

- vii   Foreword
- 1   Introduction
- **3   PART I: AN EXTRAORDINARY OPPORTUNITY**
  - 17   Ramona
  - 29   Carmen
  - 51   Glendy
  - 65   Yolanda
  - 75   Rosmery

  Artisan Groups
  - 80   Patanatic
  - 82   Totonicapán
  - 84   Quiejel

- **87   PART II: THE COLOR OF SUCCESS**

  Artisan Groups
  - 98   Chirijquiac
  - 100   Chuacruz

- **103   PART III: COLORS OF THE FUTURE**
  - 107   Bartola
  - 115   Juana
  - 119   María Ignacia
  - 127   Hilda
  - 135   Irma

- 144   Notes
- 145   Photo Credits
- 146   Alliance Organizations
- 147   Index

Introduction

Before our students embarked on their journey to the town of Panajachel for our first rug-hooking design class, some of the women, I'd been told, awoke at 3:30 a.m. They hurried through their morning chores and, lastly, made the morning meal. Leaving the food on the wood-fueled cookstove to be reheated at daybreak, they wrapped themselves in their *cargadors* (large shawls) for protection against the cool February highland air.

Their families asleep behind them, they stepped onto footpaths leading to the main road, paths illuminated by memory, for streetlights do not exist in their neighborhoods. Reaching the highway, they'd await dawn and a bus bound in the direction of Panajachel. Finally, four hours and several transfers later, they arrived at class and on time.

Arriving late, I quickly learned, is unacceptable because it conveys the message that you are ambivalent about participating in this learning opportunity. The women may not have grasped the subject matter of their class, but they were motivated by the knowledge that perhaps, just possibly, the class might help them earn money.

Entering the *sala* (classroom) by twos or threes, accompanied by their *compañeras* (friends from their village), they arrived carrying heavy bundles, some women balancing the bundles on their heads and others with bundles tied to their backs. The bundles, wrapped in colorful *tzutes* (handwoven and village-specific carrying cloths), contained their rug-hooking supplies. Some contained a baby or toddler, too. Depositing their tzutes against the wall, they pulled their cell phones out from their *huipils* (handwoven blouses), checked for messages, and exchanged brief greetings with their classmates. They wrapped their hands around warm cups of *arroz con leche* (rice milk) and accepted a tamale or two, for who can learn on an empty stomach?

Setting their empty cups aside, a polite nod and "*buen provecho*" (good health) signifies "We're ready to start." As they settled around the table, I noticed a half-dozen familiar faces from the first rug-hooking class we'd taught eight months earlier. It was reassuring to see their familiar faces because I knew the students from the first class could assist the new participants. As I checked and then rechecked my syllabus, I felt excited to jump into my lesson plans. My friend Jody Slocum distributed paper and pencils; soon we would begin to discuss ideas for rug designs.

Our interpreter and advisor that day was Deborah Chandler. Jody and I had recently met Deb in her role as director of Mayan Hands, a fair-trade craft development organization working with 160 artisans living in rural villages scattered across Guatemala's highlands. Our class roster was comprised of women from several fair-trade organizations, including participants from Mayan Hands. A quick nod to Deborah signaled the start of the class.

Deborah welcomed everyone and introduced Jody and me, and then we went around the table as the women introduced themselves. Speaking through Deb, I said, "We're going to begin with rough sketches. Think of a pattern or an object and begin to draw; it can be anything, a bird, a flower, anything." Tentatively, all the women but one, a woman named Carmen, picked up their pencils and began to scratch out lines.

Carmen, I observed, sat frozen before her paper. Her dejection was evident. Leaning toward my ear, Deborah whispered, "She's never made a mark on paper; she doesn't know what to do."

I'd prepared for this design class with a detailed syllabus organized by the hour. I'd described the class objectives and included a rationale to substantiate my lesson plan. Yet I failed to comprehend the basic skill set of my students. Unaware of it in the moment, my apprenticeship as a rug-hooking design teacher to this class of Maya women had begun.

No one observing class that day in 2010 had any reason to predict Carmen's future success because we all failed to calculate the force of this small woman's will: How she would latch on to this opportunity and alter the trajectory of her life. How she would hone her natural talent and learn to draw freehand as if born holding a pencil. How her rugs would be included among those that sold first in any collection. And how five years later she would acquire a passport, and armed with that passport, be awarded a visa following her interview with an official at the U.S. embassy in Guatemala City. How she would then fly to Santa Fe, New Mexico, to participate as an esteemed artist representing her fellow rug-hooking *compañeras* at the International Folk Art Market.

Here's how it happened.

Mary Anne Wise, Maiden Rock, Wisconsin, 2017

Part 1:
An Extraordinary Opportunity

Women Who Perform Small Daily Miracles
» Guatemala Highlands, 2007

A couple of years before volunteering to teach a weekend-long rug-hooking class, my friend and fellow weaver Jody Slocum and I spearheaded three trunk show sales of traditional Guatemalan textiles as fundraisers. The trunk shows benefited Guatemalan-based nonprofits including Friendship Bridge, a microlending organization. B.J. Bobrowski, a close friend, along with colleagues in the U.S. interior design industry participated in the endeavor.

Because Jody and I are weavers, we have a passing familiarity with the processes and the tools Maya women use to weave their *traje*, the handwoven and village-specific clothing worn by some Maya. We knew, for example, that a backstrap loom is nothing more than a complex collection of sticks and threads. Yet backstrap looms produce astonishingly intricate cloth that, removed from the loom, is fashioned into traje. The patterns on the cloth hold significance to the daily lives of Maya people and can represent creation mythology, zoomorphic figures, and other symbols associated with their village. Jody and I didn't realize that we were crafting new lives for ourselves and that the trunk shows would shape the foundation for our future.

Initially, we envisioned a single trunk show sale, but a sale with intense preparations. The preparations lasted over seven months and included a two-week collecting trip to Guatemala. After the trunk show was over, or so we said, we would return to our lives. But the first sale spawned a second sale and then a third sale in as many years. The first sale was so much work because during the process of producing the event, we learned about the extraordinary variety of traje. We also learned where to buy traje, how to decipher the woven codes or patterns embedded in the cloth that distinguishes clothing worn in one village from that of the next. We learned how to conserve the traje and how to ship it back to the U.S. And we learned how to produce the fundraiser itself. All of this presented such a steep learning curve that we told ourselves, "Of course, we should do another sale."

During the trunk show collecting trips, Jody provided logistics. She'd learned the ropes through her two-decades-long leadership role at Farmer to Farmer, a Wisconsin-based nonprofit working in Honduras and Guatemala. Her volunteer work led her to Guatemala at least twice a year where she learned Spanish and grew lifelong friendships with dozens of Tzutujil families in Santiago on beautiful Lake Atitlán. In pursuing her commitment to the people and her passion for the place, Jody began to lead tours so that Farmer to Farmer members might experience "her" Guatemala. She quickly mastered the transportation systems, discovered the locations of the country's best craft markets, and found restaurants where a tourist can eat salad with the faint expectation of not getting sick. Other incidentals were also Jody's domain—things like who will accept your personal check in exchange for local currency when none of the country's ATMs are functioning, or whom you can call to pilot a private boat so you cross Lake Atitlán right now. Possessed with an affable and perennially cheerful personality, she established connections wherever she went.

OPPOSITE: The town of Panajachel tucked at the edge of Lake Atitlán. ABOVE: Traje, traditional handwoven clothing, from Chichicastenango and Sololá regions.

An Extraordinary Opportunity

While in Guatemala collecting for the second trunk show, we reached out to some of Jody's connections with other organizations. We met Deborah Chandler of Mayan Hands, Jennifer Easter of Maya Traditions, Ramona Kirschenman of Oxlajuj B'atz' (OB), Diane Nesselhuf of Sharing the Dream, and others. We wanted to learn more about their organizations, and in particular, we wondered if any of the products these organizations produced would be suitable for our trunk show fundraisers.

We met these leaders in their offices abuzz with activity as artisans came and went, politely interrupting with a "*con permiso*" (with permission). The artisans asked questions about a product or confirmed the quantity needed to fill an order. Surrounded by stacks of colorful textiles, our eyes would dart about the room in awe of the staggering number of production hours in the handwork before us. We learned that all of these organizations were, quite simply, engaged in creating income-earning opportunities for women who had very little formal education and few options to make money.

Listening to the stories of Deborah, Jennifer, Ramona, and Diane, we began to appreciate the challenges they faced as leaders of their fair-trade organizations, such as how to gain the trust of their artisan members because the artisans are among populations of marginalized women. The artisans are accustomed to broken promises by those offering help, including the government and other nongovernmental organizations (NGOs). As trust builds, the challenge is how to lay the sequential groundwork to ensure that the women succeed in even small increments. Incremental success builds the confidence necessary to alter one's circumstance.

Handwoven cloth for sale in the market at Salcajá. RIGHT: Mary Anne and Jody with trunk show collections ready for transport across Lake Atitlán.

An Extraordinary Opportunity

To accomplish the work of gaining trust and creating opportunities for marginalized artisans to succeed, the fair-trade organizations often teach new skills. The idea is to then create products for the export market based upon the new skill. Once production standards have been agreed upon, the materials and equipment are equitably dispersed to carry out the production. In tandem with the production is assuring that the payment system is defined and transparent. Finally, the fair-trade organizations must anticipate the reception of their products in the marketplace.

I came to think of these dedicated leaders as women who perform small daily miracles. From the point of view of their marginalized clients who, among many other things, never learned to use a pencil, the rare chance to seize upon an opportunity to earn money on a semiregular basis must surely feel miraculous.

Jody and I Offer to Teach a Weekend-Long Beginning Rug-Hooking Class
» Panajachel, Guatemala, February 2009

By now, we understood that craft development associations were continually interested in expanding their array of products for the export market. New products helped them remain competitive in the marketplace and also provided some measure of confidence that income-earning opportunities for their clients might be sustained. Jody and I would be in the country collecting traje for our third, and by now final, trunk show. We reasoned that with adequate planning, we could take a weekend off to teach rug hooking if anyone was interested.

Rug hooking, I knew, would be compatible with the way the women's lives are organized. The technique is portable and, like backstrap weaving, it is easy to pick up and set down as women move in and out of a day filled with domestic duties. Equipment costs are modest and, as long as you aren't committed to hooking with wool, you could enjoy a seemingly endless supply of fabrics to hook with that could be purchased inexpensively at local *pacas*—used-clothing stores. The word paca means bale in Spanish and describes how the used clothing arrives in Guatemala from its place of origin, often the United States. Paca also refers to the used clothing itself.

Unlike backstrap weaving, rug hooking is free-form and might hold some appeal, I suspected, for those with an inventive eye. Unrestrained by the confines of the loom, I thought the students who were weavers, in particular, would understand rug hooking's free-form possibilities.

A paca shop in Panajachel.

Petronila from Quiejel holds strips of cloth cut from paca.

But rug hooking was not "of" the culture. And so before offering the class, we sought advice from those with craft development experiences. Condensing our concerns through numerous conversations, we ultimately asked, and answered, two questions:

1. Who are we to decide what a Maya woman should learn? (No one.)

2. Doesn't everybody have a right to make a living? (Yes, they do.)

It is unusual for Guatemalan NGOs to collaborate, but Brenda Rosenbaum and Jane Mintz, founders of Mayan Hands and Maya Traditions, two organizations dedicated to women's economic empowerment, decided to pool their educational resources. They formed Oxlajuj B'atz' (OB), which means Thirteen Threads in the Mayan language Kaqchikel, and hired Ramona Kirschenman as director. Throughout the year, OB conducted many workshops. The class rosters included women clients associated with both Mayan Hands and Maya Traditions coming together under one roof.

Knowing OB offered educational workshops for artisans, Jody and I approached Ramona with our idea of a weekend-long rug-hooking workshop. Ramona agreed with our assessment of the craft as a compatible fit with the way the artisans' lives were organized. She understood that the craft might have potential for income opportunities, and she liked the idea of using locally sourced paca. She enthusiastically accepted our offer to teach the workshop.

The How-Tos of Rug Hooking
» Maya Traditions Sala, Panajachel, Guatemala, June 2009

Twenty-nine women, and one man, Diego, participated in our two-day workshop. Deborah Chandler of Mayan Hands volunteered to help translate the OB-sponsored workshop. I was happy to have Deb's assistance, for she had been working with Maya women for a dozen years and had led many workshops. At her suggestion, I came up with one design, the same pattern for each participant, traced onto burlap ground cloth. Deb, who is not one to mince words, said, "Your time is short—you'll want to jump right in with the how-tos. Don't waste time explaining how to draw a pattern, just focus on the technique." And so I drew a pattern for each participant, a bird on a branch, and now with the workshop quickly underway, everybody could begin hooking. I silently blessed Deb and her good advice.

I discussed how to cut the paca into strips for hooking and how to hold the hook, and I demonstrated how to pull the strips through the grid of burlap to form loops on the surface of the ground cloth. The goal, I said, was to achieve a consistent nap height and position the loops to stand shoulder to shoulder above the burlap ground cloth. None of the women were familiar with the technique, but watching me demonstrate, a few likened it to embroidery.

Outside the classroom door, in the shade of the portico, OB fieldworkers María and Hilda assisted Jody and piled mountainous stacks of paca clothing to be used in our hooking. Reaching for the brightest clothing colors, for I've observed there is no such thing as too bright a color for a Maya woman, the students began to choose their rug colors.

As they started to hook, one student wondered if she could change the pattern. Her question, I guessed, originated from her experience as an artisan who creates products that must conform to specific standards. "Go for it," I said, and then I observed with pleasure as some freely added more design to my pattern while others simplified.

As the afternoon concluded, I anticipated that the women would be eager to begin their long return trip home. But the women, I learned, would spend the night here in the sala. OB organized dinner arrangements as part of the workshops,

Recycled cloth strips pulled through the ground cloth form loops on the surface. BELOW: Participants in the first rug-hooking class show their work.

An Extraordinary Opportunity 7

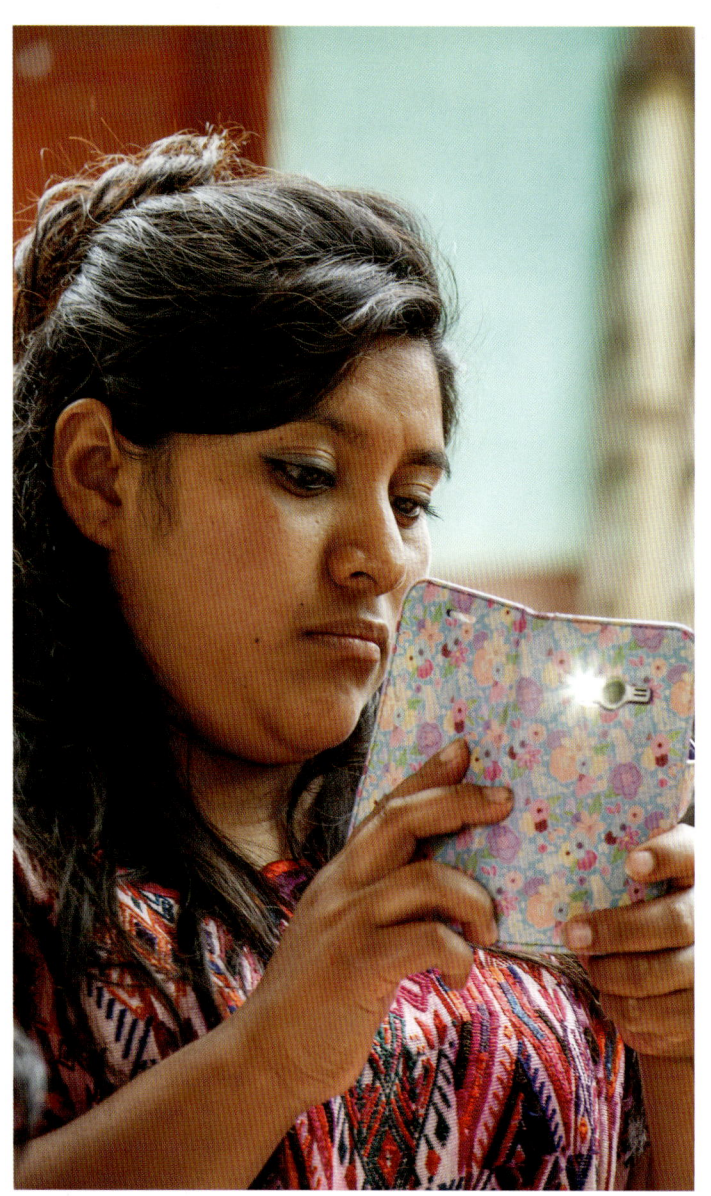

Silvia Calgua checks her cellphone, a Maya woman's lifeline. OPPOSITE: Participants in the first class working intently on their bird designs.

and a local cook would soon deliver the meal. Foam mattresses would be pulled out of storage, and the women would continue to work on their rugs until fatigued. Like women attending rug camps everywhere, I knew they would also gossip and giggle into the night.

By morning, it was evident that most had launched into their rugs without any sort of artistic inhibition. I'm convinced that lack of artistic inhibition breeds personal inventiveness, a characteristic artists everywhere admire. Inventiveness can lead to developing imagery that helps us view the world anew.

Watching them work, I noticed how quickly they adjusted to the rhythm of the process: cutting strips of cloth, then using the hook to feel for the strip hidden below the ground cloth, pulling the strand to the surface to form the nap's loop, and adjusting the tightness of their cloth to the hoop. Their hands, I observed, worked as if powered by the confidence born to a lineage of makers.

Class continued throughout the morning, and during a break, they checked their cell phones for messages. I was surprised that they all seemed to own cell phones, for I had yet to learn that cell phones were inexpensive and that cellular reception within the country is better than in most locations across the U.S. You can buy a simple cell phone for around ten dollars. You don't need a data plan; instead you buy *saldo*, or minutes, to apply to your phone in whatever denomination you're able to afford. Even if you run out of saldo, you can still receive phone calls, although you cannot place calls. The cell phone, it turns out, is a lifeline connecting to business opportunities, home, and family.

At lunchtime, Jody and I retreated to our room and Diego, the lone man in the workshop, followed us a few steps up a steep hill. Noticing the stinging ants swimming in our *agua pura* dispenser, from which we pulled fresh drinking water, he fished out the ants and boiled the water for tea on the small gas-fueled cooktop. Our hillside cabana was surrounded by a lush garden overflowing with blooming flora and some familiar medicinal plants. The sala sat below—birdsong and women's laughter filled the air. We settled onto the terrace as fragrant steam from the hot tea rose into the atmosphere around our cups. Then Diego, who I guessed was about fifty years old, told us his history as a lifelong resident of Chichicastenango.

He explained that during the civil war (1960-1996), his family and many of his friends and neighbors hid from the soldiers in the mountains. They hid for months never knowing if they would be captured, tortured, and killed. Pausing as he sipped his tea, nodding his head toward our students below he said, "They all have similar stories, you know."

Leaving our terrace and the sober conversation behind, we returned to the sala, for it was time for the "throw-down," the point in every rug-hooking workshop when rugs come off the frames or hoops. Unencumbered, the works in progress were lined up side by side on the floor for examination and admiration.

The students' rugs were alive with vivid color. Only a few of the women chose contrasting values, and their compositions positively vibrated with energy. The rugs without contrasting colors vibrated energy too, but the bird disappeared, blending into the background.

A natural at photography, Jody snapped photos of the women posing with their rugs. One woman, Carmen, stole the scene by clowning around with her classmates and inserting herself into nearly every shot. With the end of the workshop approaching, Jody took her flash drive with the photos on it to the Kodak store located a short *tuk-tuk* ride away. (Tuk-tuks are enclosed three-wheeled taxis.) She ordered prints as a gift for each woman, a memento of the class. Through her work with Farmer to Farmer, Jody understood that photographs are rare because they are an expense few can afford. She knew that a photograph documenting participation in this class would be displayed prominently in each woman's home.

Returning from the Kodak store, Jody circled the table distributing the photos as the women sat working. Exclamations of delight erupted in her wake. The women laughed with pleasure and compared their portraits.

Catching one another's eye, Jody and I understood that it was time to leave. We had appointments to keep along our collecting route. Noticing the clock, we realized that Guillermo, our private *lancha* (boat) captain, was probably already at the dock waiting to take us to San Juan. In San Juan, a community across the lake that specializes in natural dyes, we would make purchases and add to the trunk show collection.

The women continued hooking as we stood in the doorway to say our good-byes and to wish them well. And then, as if on cue, they dropped their hooking, pushed their chairs back from the worktables, and stood as one. Yolanda, a woman in her early thirties from a village near Chichicastenango, spoke first. She spoke with confidence and poise, her speech unrehearsed, straightforward, and articulate. She thanked God for the class and then she thanked God for delivering us to this place. She was grateful to learn this skill and wondered about the possibilities of this new craft, a statement left hanging in the air with no expectation of a reply.

After the fifth or sixth speaker, I felt overwhelmed by their sincerity and my eyes began to fill and then filled some more to brimming.

An Extraordinary Opportunity 9

On they continued, around the table. They acknowledged the trust their association had placed in them. Solemn promises were made to return to their group and teach what they had learned. Finally, someone sitting opposite of Yolanda picked up the thread of her statement and expressed hope that this new skill would improve their financial lives.

Two years later, Yolanda and I reminisced about that first class. She said that she felt happy to learn a new technique because learning a new technique is like someone giving you a job since there are no jobs in Guatemala, even if you have a degree. She confided that after returning home, her husband took one look at the rug in progress and said, "You've wasted your time. Who is going to want to buy something made from old recycled clothing?" Laughing, she quickly added, "He changed his mind when I started bringing home money from rug sales!"

Draw Your Own Rug Design
» Maya Traditions Sala, Panajachel, Guatemala, February 2010

My own studio work had been interrupted over the three years of trunk show sales because of the enormity of those productions. Without uninterrupted slots of time stretching before me in which to develop my compositions, I'd found it difficult to work. I'd become a stranger in my studio. But now, or so it seemed, I was to resume my life as a full-time artist. And then Ramona Kirschenman emailed to invite Jody and me back to Guatemala for a second workshop. She said feedback from the first workshop was so positive.

Did Jody and I ever pause to discuss Ramona's offer or weigh the pros and cons? I don't recall. We said, "Yes." We felt a near gravitational pull to return to work with the women, and it was a force far greater than the desire to escape Wisconsin's January weather.

Ramona proposed a five-day workshop: three days of class, a weekend-long break, and then two more days of instruction. She suggested that we further the curriculum goals by assigning homework over the break.

Responding to her suggestions, I said that my only criterion was to place the workshop emphasis on creating their own designs.

"Sounds good," Ramona replied. "Write up a plan."

The curriculum plan:
- Draw designs, enlarge to scale
- Transfer designs onto ground cloth
- Discuss color in relation to providing contrast between the elements and the field
- Troubleshoot (overpacking, underpacking, consistency of nap, and more)
- Lessons throughout to utilize design tools: direction of the hooking line and texture; how to infuse designs with energy and vitality

Rosmery cutting strips of paca.

10   An Extraordinary Opportunity

Twenty women attended our design class. We were happy to see that several students from our introductory class had returned for this class, too, including the confident Yolanda and Carmen-the-clown who had inserted herself into all the photos. The handful of repeaters would, I guessed, help ease tensions for the first-timers.

Anticipating that some of the women might complete their small rugs before the end of class—and wanting to see the rugs before returning to the U.S.—I felt eager to start hooking, but first we needed to complete the design work. We distributed paper and pencil, and I encouraged everyone to start. "Just start drawing. Think of a pattern or an object and begin to draw; it can be anything, a bird, a flower, anything. Don't worry, it doesn't matter if you can't draw. This is just a start. It's a process and it will become more familiar in time."

The women exchanged puzzled glances with one another. Then slowly, tentatively, all the women but Carmen picked up their pencils and began to scratch out lines. Carmen, I observed, sat frozen before her paper.

In response to Carmen's uncertainty, I looked to Deborah Chandler, who had again volunteered to translate, for an explanation. Carmen was aligned with Mayan Hands and Deborah had worked with her and knew her history. Leaning toward my ear, Deborah whispered, "She's never made a mark on paper. She

Ana Mariela and Yessika enjoy working together. BELOW: An early rug by Carmen Maldonado.

An Extraordinary Opportunity 11

María Sacalxot (left) and Hilda (right) help each other with drawing designs. BELOW: Drawing designs onto ground cloth was a challenging skill for many of the Maya women in the early stages of their training. A challenge they overcame quickly as evidenced by this sun drawn in the center of Silvia Calgua's rug. OPPOSITE: One of María's early rugs vibrates with energy and color.

doesn't know what to do." Deborah's statement was incomprehensible to me, yet the evidence was written in the defeat on Carmen's face.

Just minutes into the curriculum and Carmen had withdrawn into her failure. Her hands were tucked under the table on her lap and her gaze averted mine. Dumbstruck by the revelation, I wondered how a forty-five-year-old woman was unpracticed at operating a pencil. I had yet to comprehend that there was nothing about Carmen's life that intersected with the need to make a mark on paper.

Wanting to entice Carmen to participate, I riffled my mind, searching for a way to reach her. I did not want to be responsible for delivering another defeat to this small woman. I needed something to motivate her to try, but I couldn't think of what. And so, stalling for time to think of an idea, I apologized. I told them I'd forgotten an important instruction and to please put their pencils down and stand up. "I forgot to talk about where ideas come from," I said. "Let's walk around the sala and see if anyone can point to an idea to draw."

Awareness came slowly. Someone shyly pointed to the rock retaining wall and how the round rocks made a pattern of circles upon circles. One woman pointed to the scrolling iron leaves on the sala's gate, and another pointed to the quatrefoil shape of the classroom window. And then someone pointed to one of their huipils full of intricately brocaded diamonds and flowers. A few heads nodded in awareness.

As everyone sat back down, I remembered a "loosening up" drawing exercise my husband once described from his early art-student days. I'd noticed a pile of bananas near the lunch station and spaced them intermittently down the length of the table. I instructed the women to first carefully study the banana. And then when they felt ready to do so, we'd pick up our pencils—all at the same time—and everyone would have two minutes to draw the banana. Do not, I cautioned, look at your neighbor's paper. Deborah would track the time. The clock began its countdown, and groaning in misery, everyone drew the banana, including Carmen.

Deborah called "stop" and pencils were slapped onto the table as if they were poisonous snakes. I said that the next instruction was very important and to please listen carefully. With an expression on my face that read far more serious than I felt because I knew what was coming, I said, "Now pick up your drawing, crunch it into a ball, and throw it in the trash."

12   An Extraordinary Opportunity

Everyone laughed, flooded with relief and eager to be rid of that odious piece of paper. Air came back into the room. Addressing a less tense classroom and speaking through Deborah, I whispered quietly for emphasis. "I don't care if you can draw a banana and make it look real. That's not what we're doing here today. We're simply going to start drawing shapes and see what happens. Don't worry if you can't draw. Let's just begin, okay?" Everyone picked up their pencils and faced their paper.

Despite the fact that drawing was frustratingly foreign, the women kept working. Having participated in other OB artisan workshops, they were accustomed to everyone making the same product and proceeding along according to a production standard. The process in this class was confusing and unfamiliar. In this workshop, the women were able to pursue their own unique ideas. They felt uncertain and wondered, "Are we doing it right?"

The next syllabus item was a lesson on how to transfer their drawings onto rug-hooking ground cloth. I now understood that few women were familiar with a ruler, let alone possessed the numeracy skills to incrementally enlarge scale. All of us on the teaching team wanted to avoid more frustration. So with a drawing in front of me positioned next to a piece of ground cloth, I quickly revised the lesson. We would wing it. We'd simply look at the drawing and try to transfer the image on the page to the ground cloth before them.

Eventually, we began hooking and the women got into the rhythm of pulling loops and, little by little, their colorful compositions emerged. One or two designs were clearly informed by traje patterns, but most of the rugs were organic designs that vibrated with energy. The color combinations and arrangement of patterns were unlike anything I'd seen. Their extravagant use of color seemed like a proportional counterpoint to their poverty. The way they organized patterns made clear to me that they viewed the world through lenses far more complex than mine. Surrounded since birth by a world resplendent with elaborately woven garments, was it any wonder? During the first throw-down, I felt in a blink that these women were onto something authentic and rare.

In 2017, I reminisced with Carmen about this first design class. Reminding her that she didn't pick up her pencil and was afraid to draw, I asked how she overcame her fear. She grew serious and replied, "I knew I could rug hook because I'd participated in your first class. But this second class was different; we were going to make our own designs, and I was afraid to even hope I could do it. It was thanks to God I could do it because I prayed to take away my shyness and to give me more confidence."

An Extraordinary Opportunity

We're Onto Something
» Oxlajuj B'atz' (OB) Office, Panajachel, Guatemala, October 2010

The rug-hooking project may have ended there but for two chance encounters. Two rug hookers, Yolanda in Chichicastenango and Rosa in Panajachel, sat hemming their rugs in their respective local markets. A tourist settled down beside Yolanda striking up a conversation, wondering what she was sewing. The identical conversation happened with Rosa in Panajachel. Holding up the rugs, both tourists admired the work of each artisan and bought their hookings on the spot.

Within craft development organizations, nothing gets attention like sales. News of the two transactions quickly reached Ramona, the director of OB. Yolanda's compañeras soon heard the news, too, and lobbied for more classes.

Planning the next class went more smoothly because I had a better sense of how to proceed. I'd been in close touch with Ramona K. who emailed photos of the completed rugs for my critical feedback. As I studied their rugs, the direction we should take was becoming more obvious. If we coalesced as a group, within a certain framework, I reasoned we could advance their artistry and explore the market potential for the rugs at the same time. But first I'd have to explain my rationale to the women and proceed only with a consensus.

Additionally, Jody and I now had a better sense of OB's limitations. Like most Guatemalan nonprofits, funds were limited. They did not have a person on staff with the market experience or the artistic professionalism to fully explore rug hooking's potential. Ramona understood this shortfall and encouraged our leadership.

Ramona and the OB fieldworkers chose a dozen participants for the workshop. Arriving at class for this next workshop, the women quickly untied their tzute bundles and threw their rugs on the floor. Everyone crowded around, eager to examine the rugs. Jody and I immediately noticed improved craftsmanship. Their rugs were lying flatter, the women had cut their strips more carefully so the surfaces of the rugs were less frayed, and their hooking nap was more consistent.

We launched into a discussion of establishing a framework for design inspired by traje and aspects of Maya culture. Explaining my rationale, I spoke about the competitive global craft marketplace, a conversation they could relate to within the context of their own local endeavors. I reasoned that if our rugs were authentic representations of Maya culture, they would hopefully stand out on the global stage. More attention meant a better chance of success in the marketplace.

Pointing to one of the rugs with a bright and smiling sun in the sky, I asked, "Is this design unique to Guatemala?" Pointing to another rug with a house surrounded by hearts, I asked, "How about this rug. Is this design unique to Guatemala?"

Yolanda, one of the first artists to sell a hooked rug at her local market. OPPOSITE: Ramona T. hooks the border on a new rug at her home in Totonicapán where her group meets once a month to work together.

14 An Extraordinary Opportunity

Everyone agreed: "No."

Next, to drill my point home, I suggested a quick design exercise—more drawing—and this time no one protested; they simply listened with quiet attention to the instructions. I stood before them wearing my travel "uniform," a solid-colored linen shirt and skirt, and gave them two minutes to draw a rug design inspired by what I wore. Jody called "time" and the students stood to explain their drawings. Some used buttons from my shirt while others used my shirt's pocket as a pattern repeat. But their drawings were flat and lifeless. No one had much to discuss. Next I called Zoila to stand before the class. I chose Zoila because she is an accomplished weaver and every aspect of her handmade clothing is intricately detailed. The women drew another design based on Zoila's clothing. Now when "time" was called, no one wanted to stop. They kept on drawing, for they'd landed on familiar and fertile ground.

Having learned about the rug-hooking opportunity through OB, Ramona Tumax (Ramona T.) entered the program during this class. She had no prior hooking experience and said, "I was surprised to see the rugs. I'd never seen anything like them before and I enjoyed learning to make them." Within two years, her artistry had emerged, and her rug designs and craftsmanship were admired by her compañeras. In interviewing her for this book, I asked, "Did you have this artistry inside of you all the time? Were you aware of your talents?"

She said, "No one had ever commented on my work, except once in a while my husband said I did good embroidery. My friends never admired my work. Now when I come to the group and hear their comments and they describe me as an artist, I feel very good. In rug hooking, I discovered a talent for drawing I didn't know I had."

An Extraordinary Opportunity 15

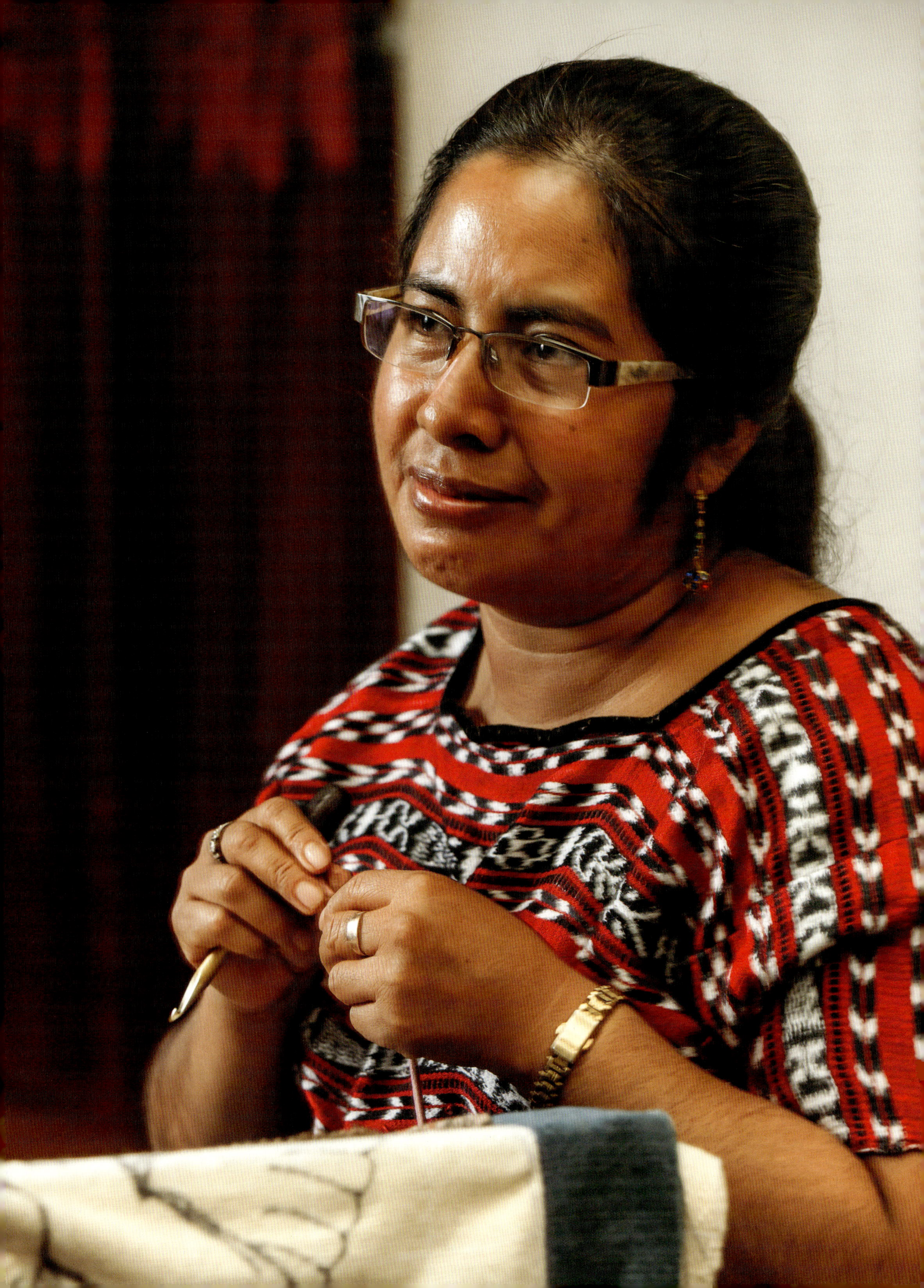

"The rugs signify our culture, but also our efforts"
» Ramona Cristina Tumax Tzunun, 39, Chiyax

As a child, Ramona made a daily two-hour trek with her family into the mountains where they collected wood and carried it home on their backs. Her mother made pottery, and the wood was needed to fire the kiln. Her father was kind, but he made clear there was no time for her to attend school. She dropped out after the second grade. Instead of attending school, her help was needed to dig the clay, make the pottery, collect the wood, and fire the kiln.

Today, Ramona lives with her husband and two children, ages four and fifteen, in Chiyax, a small village close to the city of Totonicapán. They had only been married a year

Ramona Cristina Tumax Tzunun 17

when her husband left home to find work in the United States. The plan was for him to find a job and save money. They would save money until they could afford to buy land and build a home. After a nine-year absence, he returned to Guatemala. Their plan had worked. Soon the couple had purchased a plot of land and had built a home surrounded by friends and family. Their small yard is just big enough for a couple of peach trees and a vegetable garden.

The rug-hooking project was a year old when Ramona joined the group in 2010. She recalls the first time she attended class as the "new person." "I never saw anything like these rugs before, and I couldn't believe they were made from paca material, transforming old recycled clothing. I could see that some of the rugs were very well made, and the quality of others was not as good. I was curious about them and felt hopeful I could make them, too." Ramona's critique of the early rugs typifies her ability to quickly assess the quality, designs, and craftsmanship of her peers. She would soon apply this critique to the development of her own rug-hooking skills.

A meticulous handworker, she also learned to draw and discovered a talent she didn't know she possessed. Her craftsmanship earned her a spot as one of ten participants in a later Teacher Training Course. However, shortly after joining the training program, she became pregnant and dropped out for fear that the rigor of travel might harm the baby.

Ramona Cristina Tumax Tzunun

Referring to her decision to leave the course, she said, "Even though I don't have many resources, and even though I can't read or write much, I feel like I have graduated because of my artistic accomplishments. My accomplishments have made me feel valued by others who see me as an artist. This is a good feeling because even though I didn't graduate as a teacher, I know others look up to me."

Ramona continued to pursue her craft, and soon developed a recognizable style. Today, when the rug-hooking groups converge or tour participants (see page 46) gather for a throw-down, her rugs are admired and commented upon. Her sense of color and attention to detail influence others. It is based on this sense of satisfaction and her identity as an artist that Ramona makes a point to say, "I know the value of my contributions to this project."

In speaking about her work, Ramona describes an intuitive design process. "I start to draw and then I work quadrant by quadrant, filling in the colors. And when it's done, I'm surprised at myself. In the beginning of the rug, I can't imagine how it's going to turn out, but I keep at it. And when I'm done, I say to myself, I made this, and it looks nice, and I am happy."

When asked what she hopes people see in her work, she says, "The rugs signify our culture, but also our efforts…how we have been able to get ahead. The rugs are part of us…part of our struggle to be valued, respected, and recognized. That is what we put into our rugs. I am happy to be identified with making rugs."

With income from rug sales, Ramona contributes to the household's expenses. She is saving money for her son's education and last year she bought a refrigerator. "Not on credit!" she quickly adds. "Things are more expensive when you buy on credit!" Life has improved. "My husband and I made an agreement that, for the most part, we will save my income for later. So now, unless he cannot cover a cost, we save my money."

In sitting down to interview Ramona for this book, I asked if the experience of participating in this project had changed her. Without pausing she replied, "Oh yes. Definitely. I used to feel shy. I was afraid to offer my opinion. But participating in this group with my compañeras from other communities, getting to know them, and meeting women from North America on the tours has been good. We have so much in common! These experiences have helped me to become more self-confident."

Ramona Cristina Tumax Tzunun 19

The Artist's Toolbox and an International Exhibition
» OB Office, Panajachel, Guatemala, March 2011

Early in 2011, I was invited by the Anderson Center in Red Wing, Minnesota, to curate an exhibition of hooked rugs. Along with rugs made by artists I admired in the U.S. and Canada, I included rugs by several of the Maya women.

In Guatemala, the upcoming exhibition gave us a chance to focus on raising the women's craftsmanship to exhibition standards. To celebrate the exhibition opportunity, we offered the option of working on a larger rug—24 by 55 inches—but only after demonstrating proficiency in design. The women immediately understood my challenge and instantly calculated the benefit. Hooking a larger rug meant they would earn more money, and a larger rug meant a bigger canvas for self-expression. Motivated, they greeted the news with cheers.

With Jody and OB's director Ramona translating (by now, Deb Chandler no longer assisted), I spoke about tools artists the world over use to create their works. We would learn about some of these tools during this workshop. I encouraged the women to think of these tools and processes as if they were a carpenter's toolbox. "Learn how to use these tools because this knowledge will help you become a better artist." I added that they were probably already using—or at least familiar with—some of the tools but may not have even noticed. Like most of us, once we learn a process it becomes automatic, and we don't consider it.

One of the new tools we would explore was the use of templates to help create our compositions. As we increased the size of the rugs, I knew that templates would be useful. A bigger rug meant more space to fill. Working with templates helps to envision the composition more clearly. I asked, "Have you seen artists use templates here in Guatemala?"

Someone said, "Yes, during *Semana Santa* (Holy Week) they use templates to make the street rugs." Everyone nodded in agreement. A measure of commonality had entered the room.

Next, we needed to discuss color and make some course corrections. Some of the women continued to choose consistently bright colors for all their design elements, rendering the foreground indistinguishable from the background. If they were to succeed as rug makers, they needed to adjust the color selections so the designs would be more defined and pronounced. Introducing neutral colors—to contrast with their seemingly innate preference for vibrant colors—would solve the issue.

To illustrate this object lesson, I chose one of the recently completed rugs. The rug possessed compelling elements, but the choice of background colors—identical to the colors in the elements—caused the rug to meld onto one plane. I selected a pale gray color from the pile of paca clothing and cut a few pieces of cloth as big as my hand. I invited the women to first examine the rug without the gray cloth lying on top of the background and wondered, "Do you have a reaction?" Not many commented. I suspected their eyes were accustomed to "reading" the colorful patterns used in their huipils. Their culturally calibrated eyes could distinguish the pattern from the field, but my untrained eyes could not. Still,

Alfombras (rugs) created with flowers and sawdust in the streets during Semana Santa. OPPOSITE: A good example of using gray as a background color to accentuate colorful bird designs.

An Extraordinary Opportunity

for their rugs to succeed in the marketplace, the women needed to be able to literally see my point and adjust their colors to better distinguish foreground from background.

Continuing, I arranged the gray cloth, positioning it to surround the rug's main design elements. Immediately nodding their heads, they noticed the difference, how the dull gray stood in contrast to the bright colors and the design elements popped into life. "When I placed the gray fabric next to the colorful element, did you feel the difference in your body?" They looked at me like I was crazy. No one had ever spoken to them about feeling color decisions in their bodies. But I believe in this intuitive guide; I know it to be true. From this point forward, I frequently asked the class, "Do you notice the feeling that color decision/that change of scale/that repositioning of your design templates gives your body?"

Several years later, while reflecting about the classes, I asked Carmen about this notion of "feeling the correctness of a color decision in your body." I wondered if she understood what I meant. Smiling at me with her warm, wide grin she said, "No, I never understood what you were talking about. I thought you were crazy."

But a few days later, the topic came up during a discussion with Ramona T. who said, "At first I didn't know what you meant. Then I started to notice when I was working on my rugs and now, yes, when the design is right and my colors are good, I feel it in my stomach. And it's not just rugs—it's other things, too. But hearing you say those words, about feeling it in your body, it was the first time I'd heard anyone speak like that. And now I not only feel it in my stomach— I know it in my head, too. I know when it's right."

Understanding that none of the women could afford to hook a rug that wouldn't sell, we decided to work at scale on large rug designs in preparation for the Anderson Center exhibition. We would incorporate the use of templates in our design practice and, once their designs were approved, they could transfer the pattern to ground cloth. Jody distributed paper the size of the completed rug, 24 by 55 inches. I instructed them to "find and mark the middle, so you have a reference point in placing your templates." My instructions were met with blank faces because no one understood how to find the middle of the paper. Even Yolanda, an accomplished weaver who had attended school through the sixth grade, did not understand this instruction. Art classes do not exist in Guatemala's primary school, so the women who attended grade school would not have had experience working with paper. Paper is an expense few could afford. If there is no need for paper in their daily lives, they would not have it in their homes, let alone, understand how to find the middle of the paper. Jody quickly distributed printer paper and demonstrated how to fold the paper in half first one direction and then the other. "The middle of the paper is where your folds meet," she said. They all understood and soon everyone had marked the middle on their large paper.

By now, I'd been working with the women for nearly two years. Yet in response to the find-the middle-of-your-paper exercise, I realized I was still making assumptions about their range of basic art-making experiences. Had I asked instead, "Find the middle of your warp on the backstrap loom," I am certain the weavers among them could have eyeballed the middle. From several hundred warp threads, I would bet money they could pluck the middle strand and not be off by more than one or two threads. The difference, of course, was the materials and the process. Paper versus thread; drawing versus weaving.

OB's policy was to not give away hooking materials—the women had to pay for them, albeit at a subsidized rate. If a woman could not afford the cost of materials outright, she could still receive the materials, most notably the ground cloth, and pay the money back when the rug sold. OB kept careful records and felt committed to providing this option to any of the rug hookers motivated to earn

22   An Extraordinary Opportunity

income. This was an especially enticing offer when the Anderson Center exhibit arose—and the women could create larger rugs. It meant they'd have more skin in the game, too. I was not surprised when, after having made an investment in materials and time, as their large rugs proceeded, the women frequently asked me for consultations. They were eager to learn what I thought of their rugs and wanted to know, "Do you think my design will sell?"

As a teacher, I was impressed by their genuine interest in improving their skills. Admirably, they requested forthright feedback. I'd not experienced that intensity of inquiry from any other rug-hooking students. Clearly, the women looked to me for guidance because I had a sense of the market and they did not. But as an artist, I was unaccustomed to asserting myself into another artist's design process. Yet I understood their dilemma because for most of my life, I'd made a living by what I created with my hands, too. My livelihood depended on my ability to sell my work, and so I could relate to their concern about selling their rugs. The difference, of course, was that I chose to make my living as an artist, and I always understood there were alternative ways to earn money should I fail. These women did not have a choice. Lack of income-earning opportunities was a condition imposed upon them at birth, and I knew there were no social safety nets in Guatemala.

I felt obligated to be honest and, at the same time, not get in their way. I wanted to allow space for their artistry to develop and that's the line I chose. If I thought someone was heading down a track with a lifeless design, I'd ask if she had considered expressing her idea another way. Then, utilizing a tool in her design toolbox, I asked her to demonstrate how she could alter the design.

OPPOSITE ABOVE: Sheny from the Patanatic rug-hooking group. OPPOSITE BELOW: A rug by Carmen that was featured in exhibitions at the Anderson Center in 2011 and the Textile Museum of Canada in 2013. BELOW: A rug hooked by María Sacalxot in 2011 shows a beginning mastery of the technique.

An Extraordinary Opportunity 23

I cautioned them all to avoid the pitfall of settling on their first idea. "Tease it apart, see where it leads; it's your job as artists to follow those leads."

As the rugs neared completion, it was evident that the decision to provide them with a larger format to express their ideas had worked—their rugs were sensational. They laid their designs on top of complex and expressively patterned backgrounds. I'd not seen this imagery before, and I found it exciting. I hoped their audience would also find it exciting and would purchase the rugs.

After the design consultations, my earlier ideas about creating a structured design framework to help the women design with greater confidence was growing. This framework should include not only a clear process to follow but also should be accompanied by a vocabulary for critiquing work. Like all artists, this process would help them continually evolve and self-assess their imagery. They wouldn't need to "check in" with me: they would own the knowledge.

At the conclusion of the class, Ramona, OB's director, asked me to make a special announcement. Two of the women, Yolanda and Rosa, had been chosen to travel to the U.S. to attend the exhibition opening at the Anderson Center. It was an emotional announcement, and the two artists were overcome. They never imagined this opportunity would occur in their lives. Behind the scenes, Jody, Ramona K., and I got busy and began to lay plans for ways to maximize their

An Extraordinary Opportunity

trip. We quickly went to work and teed up speaking engagements, hook-ins, rug sales, and events that would become a necessary piece of our ongoing process: fundraisers to make it all happen.

In October 2011, the rugs of eleven Maya rug hookers were included in an international hooked rug exhibition at the Anderson Center in Red Wing, Minnesota. Yolanda, Rosa, and Ramona K. attended the exhibition opening.

Reflecting on this opportunity, Yolanda said: *I felt surprised to be chosen to attend because it was something I had not imagined would really happen. My dream was to travel, and I realized that, little by little, my dream was coming true! When I learned I had been chosen to go to Los Estados Unidos, the first thing I said was that I needed to talk about it with my husband, and he said I had to make the most of the opportunity. It was the first time I traveled, and it was a nice experience. I am grateful for the opportunity because I had lots of experiences in that trip. I was scared because it was my first trip, but I will never forget it. It was the best gift I had received! I also remember the love I got from everyone I met.*

After the trip, I asked Yolanda, "What did you think about the rugs in the gallery?"

"I thought it was an opportunity for indigenous women, an opportunity to see the place because we didn't know where our rugs were sold. I saw people were valuing my work, so I gained much experience."

Then I asked, "What did you think about your fellow exhibitors—the rugs made by the *norteamericanas*?"

I saw the consistency of their rugs and realized we had a lot of work to do to become like their quality. That didn't lower my self-esteem. However, I remember I did feel a bit worried because they [North Americans] told us they had ten or fifteen years of rug-hooking experience. I thought we weren't going to be able to sell our rugs; we hadn't been rug hooking as long, but then they told me they did it as a hobby and I felt better. We don't have hobbies; we are too busy, we don't have the time to make hobbies. I also felt better when I realized their colors and designs were different and people seemed to appreciate our designs and that we used different materials, not wool. Not better, don't write that, ours were different.

An early rug by Yessika. OPPOSITE: Jody and Mary Anne working with artisans from the community of Quiejel.

An Extraordinary Opportunity

Tomasa, from the community of Quiejel, joined Multicolores in 2012. She learned to hook rugs from Yolanda Calgua. OPPOSITE: María Sacalxot enjoys hooking with her compañeras from the Chirijquiac hooking group.

Finally I asked, "Did anything else stand out for you when you attended the exhibition opening?"

"I recall there were people who even cried when they saw the rugs my compañeras and I made. That made me feel motivated. I had never seen that before. We touched their hearts somehow with our rug designs. I will never forget it."

Preparing for the Teacher Training Sessions
» OB Sala, Panajachel, Guatemala, Fall 2011–Winter 2012

After the Anderson Center exhibition, Jody and I orchestrated rug sales in the U.S. The sales motivated the women to keep making rugs because rug money was one of only a few thin revenue streams that flowed in to their households. In careful consultation with Ramona K., we divided the proceeds three ways like a pie: one-third to the women, one-third to OB to cover shipping costs and a portion of the fieldworkers' salaries, and one-third to Jody and me to cover selling expenses. Ramona, as director of OB, understood the importance of financial transparency. She also wanted the women to gain an understanding of the complexity of costs associated with their rug sales.

As sales increased and news of the project spread, more women inquired about joining the rug-hooking group to learn the technique. But our availability to teach was now limited because Jody and I had begun a new business venture called Cultural Cloth. Our mission was to represent talented and marginalized artisans from Guatemala and beyond by selling their work.

Given our limited time, and having now glimpsed the potential economic impact of this craft, Ramona K. and I discussed an idea to train a handful of the Maya women to become rug-hooking teachers. In turn, the teachers would identify prospective students in their communities.

I envisioned how the idea of training the rug hookers themselves to become teachers could build upon my interest in creating a tighter design framework. A tighter framework would sharpen the focus of design inspiration. If we trained

An Extraordinary Opportunity

the Maya rug hookers as teachers, they would need a vocabulary to critique their new rug-hooking students. An expanded vocabulary for critiques also fit with my design framework. The vocabulary would give tools for self-evaluation according to the design criteria. Thinking through the curriculum, I believed that if OB fieldworkers could travel to the communities between workshops to assess and follow up on the comprehension of the teacher training lessons, we could complete the training within a year.

Back home in Wisconsin, I prepared the syllabus for this important year of workshops. Sitting at one end of our family's long dining room table, I'd peck away on my laptop. I'd envision the objectives and lesson plans for each day and then type up a corresponding list of materials. Eventually, my gaze would drift out the bay window where my mind would unspool, and I'd think of Carmen. Carmen had been chosen to participate in the teacher training classes. I welcomed this decision. Knowing some of the obstacles she'd overcome along her path, such as lack of literacy and numeracy skills, I felt certain that one day Carmen would make a far more effective teacher than I. Yet the image of her defeat in the first design class had stayed with me and had etched a mark on my heart. I wanted her to succeed in the upcoming training. And so I considered the skills she had to possess to participate as a peer amidst her classmates. My thoughts ping-ponged back and forth. "She's a competent *cinta* (belt) weaver, but she doesn't know how to use a ruler. But as a weaver she has to measure, so what's her unit?" I determined to learn these answers and to meet her where she was, and to build upon her knowledge. If I couldn't learn these answers, I could be prepared to offer alternative routes to knowledge.

Ten women ranging in age from sixteen to fifty and representing four highland communities were invited to participate in the teacher training class. All of them eagerly accepted the invitation.

During the early years of the rug-hooking project, we worked within OB's existing group structure. From 2009–2012, OB worked with twenty groups. As was customary, OB selected representatives from these groups to attend the first rug-hooking workshop in 2009. In 2010, some but not all of the artists were replaced, extending the learning opportunity to more women. In 2011, representatives from Totonicapán joined the program. After the project established itself as an independent nonprofit called Multicolores in March 2014 (see page 72), we continued to work with the same groups and added new groups, too. Over the years, some women have dropped out of the project and others have joined. Multicolores today works with five groups from five communities.

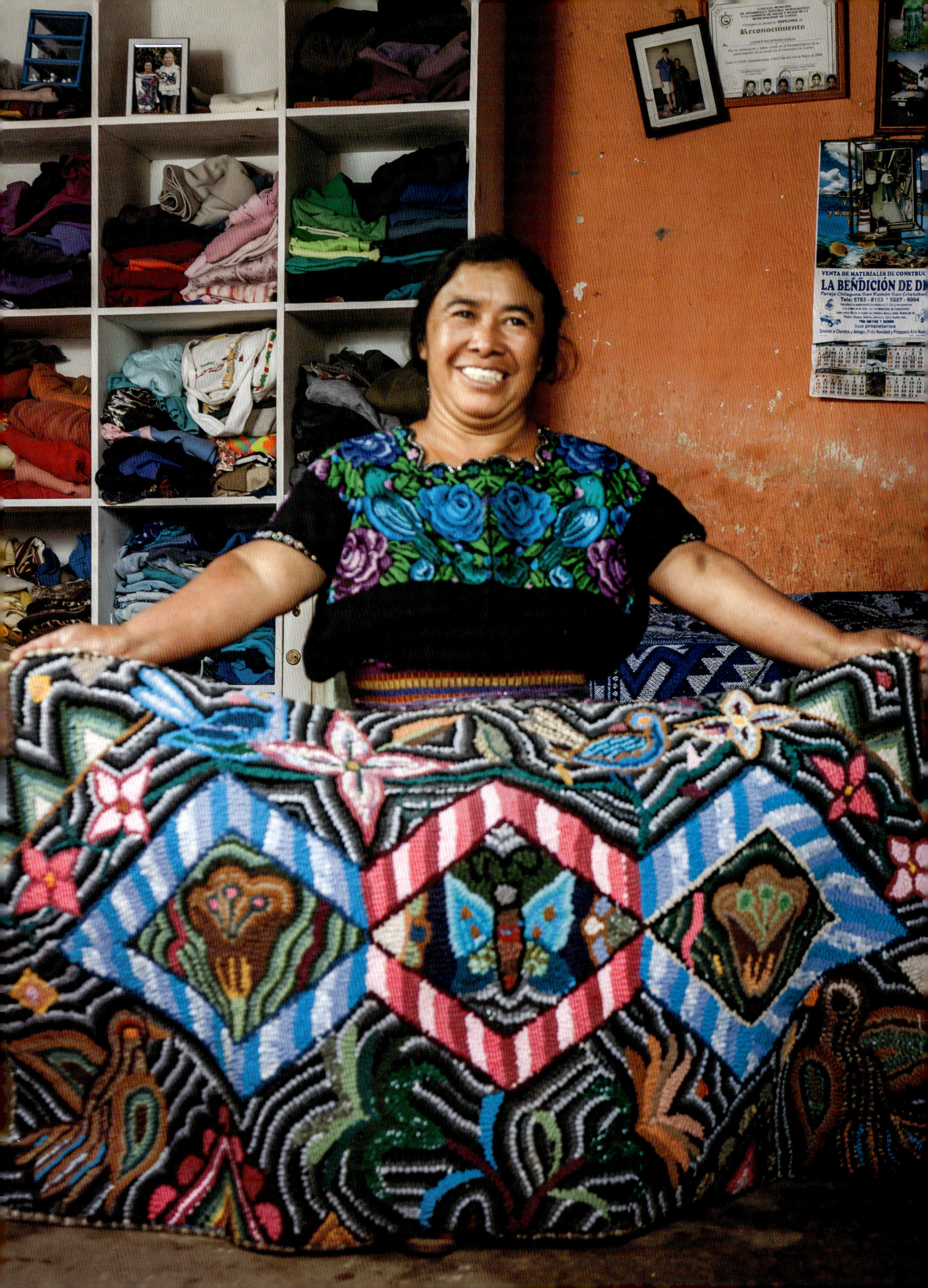
Reconocimiento
LA BEÑDICIÓN DE

"They admire me now"
» Carmen Maldonado Garcia, 53, Chirijquiac

Of all the rug hookers we have worked with in Guatemala, perhaps Carmen has overcome the most obstacles on her road to mastering the craft. Carmen participated in the very first rug-hooking class in 2009. She went on to participate in every rug-hooking class thereafter, including the teacher training course in 2012. Today, Carmen draws as if born holding a pencil and enlarges scale with an intuitive sense of design.

We would later learn that prior to attending the rug-hooking class, she had participated in many classes, hoping to find a skill that would allow her to earn an income. But nothing she learned "took." Showing up for the rug-hooking class was made all the more remarkable by the fact that she had sustained this series of defeats.

Learning of her previous failures and admiring her determination to try again to learn a skill, one day I asked her, "What made you show up for our class?"

Carmen's eyes grew large, her hands flew off her lap, and she replied, emphatically, "I was afraid to even hope I could do it!" And then she quietly added, "It was thanks to God I could do it. I prayed for help to be stronger, to give me more confidence. And you know, Mary Anne, every night I pray for the continued success of Multicolores. I pray that Multicolores continues to be successful for the women. If ever you or Reyna or Cheryl or Jody need me to help you with anything, you just ask me. I am happy to help you."

Reflecting back on her life, Carmen matter of factly describes how her mother died of alcoholism when she was nine. A few years before her mother died, Carmen had to quit school after only completing the first grade. Her brother and father looked to her to take care of the house, but she didn't know how to do the work. The extended family sent an older cousin to teach her how to cook and clean. She doesn't recall where the food came from. She married young and had three children. While their children were small, her husband wandered off. Not long afterward, she learned he had died in the street of alcoholism. Today, one son lives close by and the other two have left for the U.S. to find work.

Carmen's determination to redirect her path in life was made possible by her perseverance, motivation, and access to opportunity. She sees Multicolores as her "school," because by participating in the classes and mastering the craft, she learned new things. Participating in these activities led her to view herself as a woman capable of success in the marketplace. This change in self-perception has been noted by her family and she adds, "They admire me now."

30   Carmen Maldonado Garcia

The income from rug making and a loan has enabled Carmen to help her son buy a small plot of land. She has been able to save money, too, and is fiercely adamant about the importance of saving money. "No matter what. It is a good feeling to know that I have money to live on, and I only need to depend on myself. I don't want to ever have to rely on someone else." Her goal is to continue to save more money so as she grows old, she does not burden her children.

In early 2017, Carmen and all of the Multicolores women participated in an impact study. The study was intended to gather more information about our membership. In concluding the private interview, Carmen was asked a standard question, the same question all of the women were asked: "Do you have enough food in your house?" Carmen looked away, off in the distance. Perhaps she was remembering the past or perhaps she was searching for her reply. Returning to the moment, she said quietly, "Not always, no. I want to pay off my loan—and I won't take money from my savings. So no, I don't always have enough food."

The First Teacher Training Class: Bringing Each Other Along
» OB Sala, Panajachel, Guatemala, January 2012

Arriving in Pana (this is how locals refer to the town of Panajachel, perched on the shore of Lake Atitlán) for the first teacher training session, Jody and I were pleasantly surprised to meet the new OB staff person, Reyna Pretzantzin. Ramona K. announced that Reyna would assist with our six days of workshops. In the small-world department, Reyna had received a two-year scholarship to study at Wisconsin's Fox Valley Technical College, just a few hours from my home. She was now working full time for OB. Like many young professional Guatemalan women, Reyna spent three or four hours every Saturday commuting to a university in pursuit of her master's degree. Reyna initially attended the Antigua Campus of University of Rafael Landivar and later its Quiché Campus, attaining the title of *Licenciada*, a degree equivalent to a Master's degree in the U.S.

A little before 9 a.m. on the first morning of class, the women trickled into the sala. They greeted one another and wrapped their hands around cups of instant coffee to warm them. (Instant coffee is preferred over brewed. It's what the women can afford and is therefore familiar. It's ironic that coffee comprises one-eighth of Guatemala's gross national product, but the women cannot afford it and therefore drink instant.) Accepting a snack placed in the sala by OB, they deposited their tzutes against the wall. Some of the women had begun their trek to class at 4 a.m. Yet here they were, meticulously groomed, dressed in their best traje, and ready for the challenges of the day.

Reyna welcomed the women and began to reiterate the goals of the teacher training workshop. Stopping midsentence, she looked around the room and said, "I see you are all sitting next to your compañeras. If you are going to begin a teacher training course and become leaders, you must learn to be friendly and outgoing to your students so they can feel comfortable to learn. From now on, can we agree on a rule to not sit with your compañeras during class? Can you please sit next to someone who does not live in your village?" The women stood and repositioned themselves.

Just minutes into the class and without speaking the specific words, Reyna had set a tone to establish companionship among peers. Her timbre conveyed, "We are all equals here. And we are going to look out for one another and bring each other along."

Later, I would learn that few women have the opportunity to meet, let alone grow friendships, with women from neighboring villages. They are often isolated within their communities with little access to education and few opportunities to earn income. Additionally, lack of spoken Spanish, the language of commerce and also the language of the country's bus transportation system, provides a further isolating effect since the majority of Maya women grow up speaking a Mayan language. Only a handful of the twenty-three languages can be understood by those in other villages. Unless a rare opportunity comes along, the majority of rural women remain in their communities of birth and do not interact with outsiders. Five years after the first teacher training class, the women reflected on their cross-community and cross-language friendships.

Reyna is the youngest of seven children. Her parents are entrepreneurs and both run businesses out of the home. As a child, Reyna would sneak away and play with other kids in the neighborhood. But soon her attentive father would come find her and bring her home to help in one of the family's enterprises. Today, Reyna credits her father with teaching her a strong work ethic. Watching her parents grow their businesses inspired Reyna to one day have her own business. She viewed owning a business as a way to be independent, but she didn't have the money to start a business. Attending university part-time on Saturdays meant that she could work during the week to support her ongoing educational pursuits. One day, she saw OB's job description advertising the position to manage its store stocked with artisan products. Scanning the applicant requirements, she realized she might possess the necessary experience. She spoke English, she had experience working in her family business, and she had experience managing production through her work history at two different stores, Mercado Global and Nim Po't. She liked the idea of working with artists but felt a bit intimidated to think she would have to manage groups, manage quality control, and innovate new products. After accepting the job offer, she felt relieved to learn that Jennifer Easter, director of Maya Traditions, one of two NGOs that founded OB, would mentor Reyna for a specified time period. At first, Reyna was not involved in the rug-hooking project, but she saw possibilities and voiced an interest in participating more directly in the program. Ramona recognized that if Reyna was to assert her authority as OB's store manager responsible for quality control, including the rugs, then Reyna must be assigned a greater role in the project.

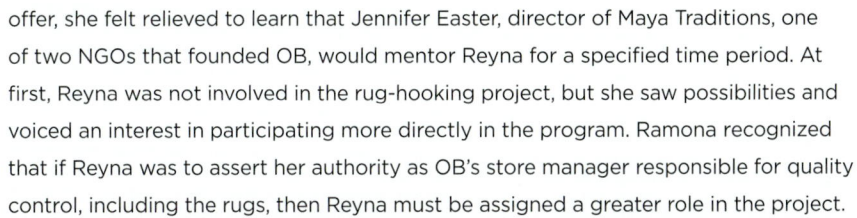

An Extraordinary Opportunity

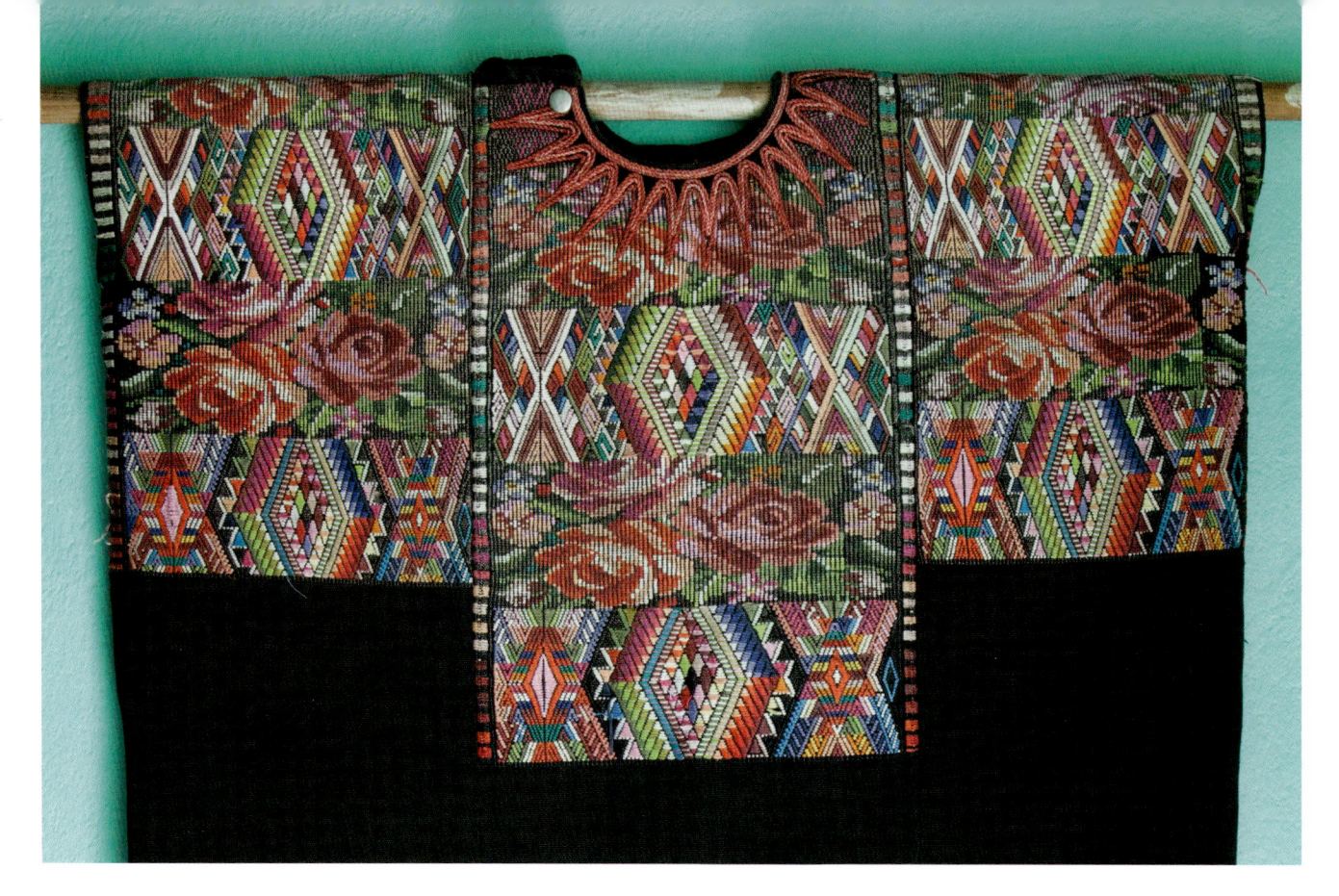

A gorgeous huipil reflects an aesthetic of Guatemalan textiles that inspires the design framework for the Multicolores rug-hooking artists. OPPOSITE: Mary Anne critques rugs from the Totonicapán rug hooking group.

Glendy said, "I like getting to meet many more people and growing friendships. It is good to talk and communicate and learn from each other when we get together in class. Without this program, I wouldn't have had an opportunity to meet women from other villages."

Ramona T. opened her arms as if to embrace her compañeras and laughed at my question as if to say, "Don't you know anything? Mariana! It would not be possible to know these women without the project. I never thought I'd have the opportunity to meet women like these—and this is one of the parts we like the most."

That first morning, we discussed what made a good teacher. I said, "Even if you never attended school, somewhere in your life someone has taught you. Maybe an aunt, a grandmother, or a neighbor." I asked about the characteristics of a good teacher and the women freely offered their opinions.

"When I have a good teacher, I want to copy them." "A good teacher makes you feel good in your heart." "With a good teacher, my heart felt like a glass of water—so full!" And finally, "A good teacher wants you to succeed." Reyna added, "From this day onward let us agree to proceed as good teachers."

Next, we discussed the tools in their "design toolboxes." I asked, "As artists, what is the most important tool in your toolbox?"

Someone said, "A good work ethic." "Good combination of colors." And then, "Our creativity."

I asked, "Can a person who has never been to school open her mind to new ways of doing things?" María Sacalxot nodded yes. I followed up with "Can a person who can't read or write learn the creative process?" They nodded their heads in agreement. I concluded by saying, "Your mind is your most important tool. It does not matter if you've never been to school."

With several new participants in the class, Reyna and I felt it was important to reassert the decision to coalesce our design framework around traje, so we reviewed the rationale that their rugs reflect their textile heritage. Our rug designs should look as if they could only have come from Guatemala.

34   An Extraordinary Opportunity

We also reviewed the value of templates in the design process. I explained how artists the world over create a repository of templates. "They create the same template in a variety of scale to be used and reused over the course of a lifetime. You'll want to begin to grow your own collection of templates—like a library of ideas. It'll save you time because you don't have to continually redraw your images. Any questions?" No one spoke so we moved on.

The next topic to introduce was the critique process. Reyna knew we had to explain the rationale for critiques in the curriculum or the women would not take it seriously. She also knew that constructive criticism is not a familiar practice within the culture, hence our care in introducing the topic. In addition to making them better teachers, Reyna knew that the critique process could help pave the way for establishing quality standards and provide the accompanying vocabulary. Introducing the subject, I said, "Listen carefully to our next topic because not only will this process help you become a better artist and teacher, it will also help you with your husbands!" That got their attention.

We explained that as teachers they must help their students improve their designs and their craftsmanship. Reyna said, "We realize it's difficult for most people to accept criticism. But remember, a good teacher wants her students to succeed. A good teacher wants her students to hook rugs that have a chance to succeed in the marketplace. As teachers, it will become necessary for you to offer constructive criticism. If you present the criticism in a specific way, it will help your students (or your husbands) hear what you are suggesting. Mary Anne and I will now demonstrate how to deliver constructive criticism. Please pay attention because when our demonstration is over, it will be your turn to demonstrate in front of the class." The women listened, a bit wary, not sure what was coming next.

Reyna and I demonstrated the critique process. I played the student and Reyna played the teacher. I showed her my hastily sketched rug design, drawn for the purpose of role-playing, and she responded offering very specific praise. "Oh, I can see this design is inspired by a huipil from Patzun, yes? I love their huipils, especially the way they embroider feathers around the collar. But may I make a suggestion?"

I said, "Sure, I came to you for help."

Reyna continued. "What would happen to your design if you varied the scale of your feathers? How do you think that would change it?"

Feigning ignorance I said, "I don't understand what you're saying. Can you show me what you mean?" At that point Reyna picked up scissors and paper and began to make templates of my feathers in a variety of scale. She positioned and repositioned the templates around my drawing.

Turning to the class we asked what had just happened in our exchange. Slowly we identified the steps: (1) offer specific praise, (2) ask permission to make a suggestion, and (3) offer specific suggestions for improvement and be ready to demonstrate your suggestions.

To become more familiar with the critique process, we role-played one more time in front of the class. Reyna chose Delores as the teacher and once again I was the student. Reyna's choice was not lost on me because we both knew Delores was a quick learner and a good artist. But we also knew that others felt intimidated by her

An Extraordinary Opportunity 35

serious personality. Delores rarely smiled, and she was quick to criticize. I showed her my design, and she immediately launched into criticism, forgetting to say something positive and specific and forgetting to ask permission to make a suggestion.

I turned wordlessly to the class, searching their faces for a reaction to Delores's critique. As a group they shook their heads and told Delores where she'd gone wrong. Delores tried it again, and this time she passed. Then we divided the class into pairs and Reyna and I observed their critique exchanges.

Around the room we went. In previous classes, Carmen acted the clown, but now, in performing the role of teacher, she had become insecure. Examining her student's design, she barely spoke above a whisper. Her student had to strain to hear her. She briefly addressed her student's work sample saying the design was pretty and no changes were necessary. She quickly returned her student's drawing as if she felt uncomfortable holding the paper. Intervening, Reyna said, "Carmen! Talk louder! Pretend you're telling a joke! People want to hear what you have to say." But Carmen was unaccustomed to providing constructive criticism to a peer. She needed more practice.

Mary Anne and Reyna team teach with extraordinary intuition about the artists and each other. OPPOSITE: A dazzling rug by María Estela Az Tamayac reflects perfectly the Maya design aesthetic.

Glendy, with her youngest baby Dulce María asleep in a tzute tied to her back, played the role of teacher and welcomed her student by name. "Nice touch," I thought, because it felt personal and put the student at ease. Glendy offered specific praise and asked for permission to provide feedback. She engaged the student in conversation and listened with respect. She suggested simplifying the design and picking up the scissors, she offered to cut more templates. She concluded by saying, "If you have any problems, I would be happy to come to your house and give you more help."

At the conclusion of the role-playing exercise, we gave ourselves a long round of applause.

Observing Glendy in this interchange, I thought to myself, "I bet she's a great mom," and as I got to know her, I learned it was true. One day while visiting her home, I saw storybooks for her children. I had not seen storybooks in any of the women's homes before or since. The vision of those books has stayed with me. Glendy is a woman with few resources, yet she placed a high enough value on books to make them a part of her household. Several years later, I asked Glendy about her thoughts on learning the critique process.

"The process helped to create a vocabulary which helped us improve our rugs. I learned about constructive criticism, which I didn't know about before. The process has been useful in other areas of my life, too."

The budget for the six days of classes included travel expenses for the women because most of them lived at too great a distance for a daily commute. Participating in the teacher training classes meant they would spend the nights at a nearby hotel. For some of the women, like sixteen-year-old Rosmery, not only was this the first class she'd attended with adult women, it was her first time away from her home and family. The students ate their meals at local restaurants and were able to order meat at each meal—at home they might eat meat once a week. Accustomed to working long hours, attending classes away from home meant freedom from domestic duties and a chance to unwind a bit and grow friendships with their classmates. After dinner, they'd walk up Santander, Panajachel's main street full of tourists and street vendors and open-air cafés, where music spilled onto the street and into the night. Homework was assigned every day, and like rug camps everywhere, the women worked and laughed and gossiped into the wee hours.

Back in class, the morning began with an overview of the day's objectives followed by homework review and a discussion of stumbling blocks. Over and over, we repeated that everyone learns at her own pace. "If you're a mother with more than one child, then you know this is true for you have observed how each of your children learns differently. You may find today's lesson is easy for you but difficult for your friend. Tomorrow's lesson may be difficult for you and easy for your friend. We'll proceed along together. You simply need to do one thing: practice, practice, practice."

As co-teachers, Reyna and I were learning about each other, too. We quickly tuned in to reading, if not anticipating, one another's thoughts. So when two of the students, Yolanda and Zoila, showed up without their homework, a glance at Reyna told me what was coming. She sent the two outside the classroom and politely but firmly explained that they could rejoin us when their homework was finished. Message delivered, I knew, and every student heard it.

The afternoon's lesson was to prepare for our daylong field trip to the Museo Ixchel, the only official textile museum in *La Capital* (Guatemala City), located on the campus of Francisco Marroquín University. None of the women had been to

In early 2017, I asked several of the women, "How frequently do those living near you eat meat?" Yolanda said that her family (her husband and two teenagers) has meat four or five times a week. She knows that most of the people who live in her community eat meat once a week and some less than that. Glendy said it was common for most of the people she knows to eat meat once a week and always on Sunday. She added that in her family of nine, they eat meat at least once a week. Pointing in the direction of nearby Lake Atitlán she added, "We also eat fish. Meat is expensive, around Q35 a pound (about $4.50 per pound), and I know people who eat meat maybe once a month."

An Extraordinary Opportunity

A booth along Santander Street in Panajachel filled with tipica.

the museum, and only one of them had been to La Capital. To most rural women, their impression of La Capital is unfavorable. It is a dangerous place full of gangs and crime and should be avoided if possible. Urban myth or not, they had all heard of people who traveled to the city, where something bad happened and the person never returned. I assured them we would be safe and would travel together in our own van. Still, the women felt anxious.

My rationale for visiting the museum was to experience a point of pride in an "official" establishment dedicated to honoring Maya textile traditions, both past and present. If they experienced a museum dedicated to their textile heritage, perhaps they would begin to understand the value of Maya textiles to the society of the world. Making another leap of logic, I hoped the experience of viewing their textiles in a museum would drive home the rationale behind choosing traje as the framework for rug designs.

In preparation for the museum visit, we talked about the importance of sketchbooks to capture ideas and inspiration. I explained that at the museum they would see many textiles they'd not seen before, and these pieces could become the basis for designs. I relayed how artists around the world make a habit of carrying a small sketchbook because one never knows where or when ideas will come. If you don't sketch the ideas, you will likely forget the image. We distributed small drawing tablets and to practice sketching in the notebooks and to overcome any shyness about drawing in public, we left the sala.

Together, as a class, we walked down Santander, jammed with tourists, mobile food stands, restaurants, itinerant vendors, shops, and stalls selling *tipica*. Tipica is a word used to characterize a wide array of trinkets for the tourists: beaded jewelry, crudely crafted purses, poorly woven table runners, crocheted balls for juggling, crocheted water bottle carriers, and more. One stall after another inexplicably offered nearly the same array, and all day long the vendors call out

38   An Extraordinary Opportunity

to passersby hoping to lure them in for a closer look. Not realizing that Jody and I were accompanying the women with the sketchbooks, the vendors urgently called to us "*Adelante!*" (Come in!) or "*Que le gusta?*" (What do you like?). Occasionally, a stall displayed a collectible that merited a closer look—an unfamiliar huipil representing a community tradition not seen before or a huipil that was a new iteration from a familiar locale. These pieces caught the women's attention and were sketched in their books.

In planning our field trip to the Museo Ixchel, we'd reached out to Barbara Knoke, a cultural anthropologist recently retired from her role as acting curator of the museum. When asked if she would meet our students and lead the tour of the exhibition she said, "Yes." The exhibition on view was the same as when I'd first visited the museum four years earlier. The Museo, I learned, is funded only through private donations and operates on a shoestring. (It is ironic because at the airport in La Capital, tourists arriving in Guatemala are greeted by posters of indigenous women wearing traje. The posters feature women weaving on backstrap looms with picturesque Lake Atitlán in the background. The weavers on the posters appear as if they don't have a care in the world. The same government that entices tourists to "come and see indigenous weavers" can't find money to help support a museum dedicated to the country's textile heritage.) Greeting us at the museum's entrance, Barbara put the women at immediate ease with her warm welcome. They felt free to ask questions and free to sketch in their notebooks, but they were disappointed that they couldn't take photos with their phones. As Barbara chose huipils from the museum's collection for the women to examine more closely, they noticed that before extracting the garment from a storage drawer she first pulled on white gloves. Her caution did not go unnoticed, as the women elbowed one another in surprise of Barbara's concern.

Leaving La Capital behind us, en route to Pana we stopped in Antigua, the lovely former colonial capital and a UNESCO World Heritage Site. Noted for its cobblestone streets and its colonial ruins, Antigua attracts visitors from all over the world. Tourists enjoy the many open-air restaurants, live music, and great shopping. And it was the high-quality, handwoven textiles in a few of those shops that I wanted the rug hookers to see. I wanted the women to absorb the details of quality work. It didn't matter that we were looking at textiles rather than rugs. The quality of the braided trim on a bedspread, or the flawless sewing on a pillow with a hidden zipper was evident. If we were to enjoy success in the marketplace, we'd have to aim high with our craftsmanship, too.

I should have made prearrangements to visit the shops because, unlike our experience with Barbara Knoke at the Museo Ixchel, we were not made to feel welcome in the stores. I immediately regretted my lack of forethought. Competition for tourist dollars is fierce, and the shop owners likely felt we were there to steal ideas. In spite of my hasty explanation, one of the shops refused us entry. Had Jody and I been by ourselves and not accompanied by eleven Maya women, there would have been no problem.

Walking down the street in Antigua, I fell in step with Rosmery and took advantage of the moment to inquire why she wasn't in school. She repeated several times that she was in school. And then it dawned on me: rug hooking training is her school. Continuing on, she explained, "I like seeing new and different things—all these places I'd heard of before and never thought I'd see in person. It's inspiring and I am getting many ideas!"

Iglesia de La Merced. OPPOSITE: Ramona T., Reyna, and Carmen confer about design and color choices.

Ending our field trip on an upbeat note, we stepped out of the hot bright sun and crossed the thick threshold of the *Iglesia de La Merced*, the Church of the Mercedarians, a male monastery order of the Catholic church. Entering the cool and subdued narthex, with its vaulted ceilings and nave stretching before us, light spilled down from the windows recessed in walls three feet thick. We grew sober taking in the splendor, for La Merced is a beautiful example of seventeenth-century baroque architecture. Reyna understood that the women would enjoy seeing this sanctuary, for she knew none of them had experienced such an awe-inspiring place of worship. Soon they were lighting candles, adding to the dozens already burning on a shelf before the Virgin Mary in her small, intimate alcove. First dripping wax onto the shelf and positioning the candles to stand, they crossed themselves and offered prayers of petition. They blessed one another, Jody, Reyna, me, OB, Ramona K., and our journey. Their most fervent petitions asked for blessings as rug-hooking teachers.

On the drive back to Pana, I discussed the weekend's homework. I told them, "Come to class with two completed rug designs drawn at scale and inspired by something you saw at the museum. You must be prepared to demonstrate how you came up with the designs through use of templates. You and the partner Reyna chooses for you will practice the critique process for the review in front of the class." Letting my announcement sink in a moment, I followed with the now familiar, "Any questions or comments?" No one spoke. Continuing, I said, "Whose responsibility is it to have all the materials you need in order to complete the homework?" No one answered because by now they'd heard the question many times and recognized the subtext: don't come to class empty-handed.

The instructions were met with silence. It was going to be a lot of work, and I could see their minds calculating. Having been away from home to attend class for the past three days, their domestic chores had accumulated significantly. But I could also see idea wheels turning as a few of them opened their notebooks and began to draw.

At class on Monday morning, sitting next to their village compañeras, it was clear everyone was eager to get started. Reyna, after asking them to reposition themselves and sit next to someone other than a village friend, provided a rundown of the day's agenda. Over the weekend, she had created a monitoring form and was explaining the form to the women. The form, she said, was to help us assess how well they understood the critique process and their homework assignment. We would listen to their critique sessions and look at their designs and mark our forms to determine if they had followed the instructions. With this information, we would be able to focus on those who needed additional help. She reminded them that to become good teachers, they must understand what we'd covered thus far. This last piece of information—focusing on becoming good teachers—helped the women accept the news that they'd be graded.

An Extraordinary Opportunity

Later, we would use the monitoring forms and expanded versions of the form any time we introduced a new process or reviewed complex homework assignments. The forms revealed precisely what Reyna intended and identified who needed more help. It often fell to Jody to sit with the students who needed additional review.

We wanted the women to hear from someone with high-quality production standards and global sales experiences, so we invited Olga Reiche who agreed to speak to our class. Olga is a Guatemalan woman who works with women in Cobán who weave *pijbil*—a delicate, gauzelike cloth. She also works with natural dyers in San Juan and with *ixcaco* farmers. Ixcaco is a species of naturally colored cotton in browns, mauves, and even sage green. It had been supplanted by coffee, which at the time was a more profitable crop. Ixcaco had nearly become extinct. Today, it's been rediscovered by high-end textile producers and is slowly being reintroduced.

Olga is a warm and friendly woman with a broad knowledge of textile practices. She spoke about old huipils woven from ixcaco and how the huipil colors were not so bright as they are today. The reason, Olga said, was because they used ixcaco, a cotton with a natural brown or mauve color. The rug hookers had just learned this at the Museo and were able to comprehend the value of Olga's motivation to grow ixcaco to preserve a tradition. Olga reinforced our rug-design framework, too. Drawing upon her marketing experience, she said, "Your rug designs should look as if they could only have come from Guatemala." Yolanda asked her about her sales experiences outside Guatemala. Olga said, "The U.S. is a very good market. The weavers I represent sell their traje at a fair called the International Folk Art Market in Santa Fe, New Mexico."

The women understood the concept of a "good market," but connecting to that distant market seemed as remote as the moon.

Finally, we turned our attention to their design homework. It was immediately evident that everyone was tentative in their approach to incorporating a variety of scale and use of traje in their designs. We'd covered how to do so in class, but exchanging looks with Reyna we both understood it was time to review. We needed to convey specific steps in the process that detailed design principles as guidelines to follow.

Remembering how Reyna presented the critique information framed in the context of "When you become teachers..." I decided to adopt the same approach for the discussion on design principles. We had discussed the principles before and we thought they had been understood. Looking at their homework, we now knew that we needed to review the principles as a class. I said, "When you teach others, it is likely that you will have students who cannot read or who can only

Illustrations of the six design principles.
OPPOSITE: Yolanda's rug with twenty-two different birds served as a resource for practicing templates and design principles.

read a little. To help your students better understand the principles, let's create small drawings in our notebooks to represent these ideas. The drawings will help your students to understand and remember the design principles." Walking to the whiteboard, I asked, "Who can draw something to represent principle #1, 'Our designs must come from traje'?" Glendy suggested a huipil, and came to the board to draw it. "What about avoiding things that are common?" (The word "trite" does not exist in Spanish and so we settled upon "common.") Carmen, who does not read, came to the board and sketched a house. Smiling, she made a big X through it. We continued through the six design principles until we had icons to represent each concept.

1. Create designs extracted from elements of traje.
2. Avoid using things that are common or objects and symbols that can be found anywhere. We want our rugs to look like they could only have come from Guatemala.
3. You can combine figurative images—like birds on huipils from Santiago—with geometric elements—like diamond designs found on huipils from Santa María de Jesus.
4. You must vary the scale of your design elements.
5. Your design must possess energy and vitality—its own life force. Principle #4 can help achieve this.
6. The dimension of your border must be in proportion to the size of your completed design.

To become more familiar working with the design principles and templates, and indeed the entire artistic process, we replicated a rug Yolanda brought to class. Inspired by a huipil from Santiago, her rug contained twenty-two birds in a variety of scale. We traced the birds to create templates and divided the class into teams; each team had the same set of the twenty-two bird templates. The teams positioned and repositioned their birds until satisfied with the composition. Next, they traced the birds onto a large sheet of paper, the paper representing the size of the finished rug, and this is called "drawing at scale," I said. Pinning the designs in progress to the wall, we noticed how each design was different, even though they started with the same "information." As they were busy pinning their drawings to the wall, a practice that was now familiar, I'd collected some of their templates, choosing those of the exact same size. Pinning my piece of paper to the wall, I positioned my same-sized birds around the page. We compared their drawings of various scaled birds to my drawing using birds all the same size. The difference was obvious. My design was lifeless. "Which design principal did I forget?" I asked. They answered, "#4 and #5."

42   An Extraordinary Opportunity

While still on the topic of design principles, I wanted to review principle #3, "Combine figurative with geometric imagery." I told them, "You've used your bird templates very well. You've arranged your templates using variety of scale and your designs possess energy. It's evident that you have followed design principles 1, 4, and 5. I'd like you to carefully review the design principles before answering the following question. How do you intend to render your birds? Will you hook them in solid colors? Will you make them look realistic? Or…?" Everyone immediately grasped that according to design principle #3, they could incorporate geometric traje patterns within the realistic forms of their birds.

The design principles would be reviewed over and over until everyone could refer to their meaning without notes. Years later, when asked about the design principles and if they helped her, Glendy replied, "I had never considered these ideas before, and I still use them in all my rugs. Before the principles, my approach to rug design was kind of scattered—I was guessing—but the principles gave me confidence. I became more sure of myself. I use these when I teach or when one of my group has a design problem, we talk about the principles."

Having completed the object lesson, the women eagerly got to work. After tracing their templates onto their ground cloth, they chose their rug colors. Pulling apart the pile of paca fabric, comparing a handful of fabrics in one hand to those

LEFT TO RIGHT: Bartola cuts paca. Irma hooks a rug in front of a huge pile of paca. OPPOSITE: Zoila, guided by innate artistic abilities, selects, slices, and shapes a variety of paca for her rugs.

in the other hand, they made decisions along the way. Fingering the fabrics, they tested the suitability of their selections, for they'd become expert at choosing a knit shirt over a sweatshirt, for example. They had learned that a sweatshirt, unless well worn, is too thick, making it difficult to pull through the ground cloth. Flannel pajamas or a tee shirt are preferable to a cotton skirt that frays when cut into strips. Tug on the cut flannel or tee shirt strip and it rolls into a wormlike tube. Hooking with "rolled" strips means the surface of the rug will be smoother, less frayed.

While digging through the pile, Carmen found a few yards of lace. She placed it on her head like a mantilla and with hands folded in prayer, to everyone's amusement, she took a somber stroll around the classroom.

Throughout the afternoon, informal conversations arose. Rosmery complained that after our field trip and design discussion, she now had so many rug ideas she couldn't sleep. When she closes her eyes she sees rug designs. Riding the bus home, she sees rug designs. Everyone concurred, chiming in with their own stories. Yolanda added that the design principles have informed her backstrap weaving, and she is now playing with scale on the brocaded elements in her cloth.

Rummaging through the paca pile and selecting rug colors, Carmen pulled me aside to ask feedback on her choices. Feigning ignorance, I asked Zoila to perform the role of Carmen's teacher.

I chose Zoila because I wanted another opportunity to observe her artistic process. I'd watched her at work in previous classes and concluded that for a woman with no prior experience handling art materials, she uses the tools with an inexplicable familiarity. Her design ideas seemed to flow from her head to the page effortlessly as if she were eyeing the world through a visionary lens. She'd examine a huipil I'd pinned to the wall for inspiration and then she'd return to her chair and condense the essence of the woven pattern into a rug design. The result was at once compressed and expansive. Compressed for she'd condensed the essence, expansive for she portrayed the familiar in a way not seen before.

Zoila is quiet and soft spoken, and while it's clear to me that she is gifted, she doesn't consider herself exceptionally talented. Often shy in class, she joins the conversation only when prompted. I suspected her approach to color is intuitive, and so as I watched her interact with Carmen, handing Carmen her color suggestions, I interrupted to remind her that her role is to teach. "Please explain your choices. Why do you recommend burgundy?" I asked.

Very quietly she replied, "It contrasts well with her lime green." Pointing to a bird, she said, "It also relates to the pink she used here, only it's more saturated." She had learned the vocabulary to articulate her color choices in class and listening to her words, it was clear she'd connected her new lexicon to her process. Satisfied, Carmen thanked her for her advice and returned to work.

As our first teacher training session began to wind down, Reyna made two announcements. The first announcement was that in cooperation with Jody and me, OB would sponsor a rug-hooking tour that would take place the following month.

Over the next few weeks, Reyna would help the teachers-in-training prepare to welcome rug hookers touring Guatemala from North America. All the women but Yolanda exchanged nervous glances as if to say, "What have we gotten ourselves into!" Speaking all at once they said, "We don't speak English! How will we interact?" But Yolanda, through her work with Maya Traditions, had experience with *extranjeros* (foreigners), and she alone welcomed the news. Advising her compañeras, she said, "We cannot predict the relationships that can grow from this visit. I think it's a good idea." Then, exposing her entrepreneurial roots she added, "Who knows? The extranjeros might even want to buy your rugs."

An Extraordinary Opportunity

The Language of Rug Hooking

The tour would pair ten norteamericanas with ten rug-hooking Guatemaltecas. In order to achieve a one-on-one tour participant to Maya woman ratio, the ten teachers-in-training were invited to participate on the tour. Reyna and OB's director Ramona wondered if the husbands and *suegras* (mothers-in-law) of the teachers-in-training would support the women and take over their domestic duties while the women were away from home on the tour. But all ten Maya women were able to participate. With Reyna's assistance, they prepared to meet their North American rug-hooking buddies.

Reyna, with the experience of traveling to the U.S. as a scholarship student still fresh in her mind, understood how daunting international travel can be. She also understood how intimidating it can be to communicate with those who do not speak your language. With these experiences in mind, she was determined to create a welcoming environment for both the norteamericanas and the Guatemaltecas participating on the tour. In the weeks following the first teacher training, Reyna gathered the Guatemaltecas together and they planned welcoming activities and discussed how to watch out for everyone on the tour, not just their paired buddies. She also gave culturally sensitive tips like "Don't ask the age of your buddy." She told the women that we want everyone to make friends, to connect with one another, and to have a great time. During this planning session, the women soon created an agenda for the week's rug-hooking activities that included helping their buddies design a rug the "Maya way."

On the first tour in February of 2012, sixteen-year-old Rosmery was paired with Peg, a high school art teacher from Red Wing, Minnesota. With her sunny smile, Peg embraced Rosmery's design suggestions as the two collaborated on Peg's rug. As the days progressed, in spite of language barriers, we watched Rosmery and Peg interact. Rosmery blossomed. Carmen, nervous to begin the tour, was paired with eighty-year-old Jean from Mankato, Minnesota. Jean, in spite of having hooked for several years, patiently complied when Carmen insisted that she pull out loops that weren't to her standards. By the end of the first day, we noticed Carmen relax and giggle with Jean. Six days later, as the tour concluded, it was clear to all watching: the two had forged a friendship that informed both of their lives.

Jean and Carmen work side-by-side on the first rug-hooking tour.

Growing friendships, overcoming shyness and boosting confidence, sharing rug-hooking tips and coming together united in purpose, that is what the tour was about. The norteamericanas gained insights about their compañeras' lives and a deeper appreciation for the Maya women's artistic accomplishments. To this day, rug-hooking tour alumni from Texas to Washington to Canada and the East Coast are among Multicolores's most loyal supporters. They are our champions.

In 2017, I asked a handful of women about their thoughts on the rug-hooking tour.

Carmen replied, "That first tour I was nervous, I'll admit that. But it helped me to realize I didn't have to speak English, which would've been impossible, you know. It was pretty amazing, really, how the language of rug hooking took over. I also knew everyone else was nervous, even the norteamericanas. I felt very happy to discover I'd worried for nothing. It was actually a lot of fun. I really like all my tour buddies."

Ramona T: "The Guatemaltecas get to know a new location. And we share experiences with our extranjera students even though we can't speak English and they do not speak Spanish. It's a good experience; it makes your heart feel good to meet the tour women. I am happy to be included on the tours."

María Sacalxot: "The tours are a good idea because we see different ways of working and using color, too. Working with the extranjeras has helped me overcome my shyness, and I'm now more comfortable expressing myself. That is a good feeling. I also like getting to know new cities and getting to know my way around them."

Zoila helps Jen with rug designs on the 2013 rug-hooking tour.

With an eye on the clock and their thoughts turning toward their long return trip home, the women began to pack up their supplies. They grabbed last-minute color choices from the paca pile and folded them in their tzutes. Some used their cell phone's camera to photograph an instruction taped to the wall. As usual, Glendy, with Dulce María dozing in a tzute tied to her back, was first to find the broom and sweep up the detritus of colorful snippets and paper scraps scattered like confetti throughout the sala. Working together the women cleaned the room, organizing the recycled materials, stacking the chairs, and wiping the tables. Mixed emotions ruled their faces. They were exhausted by all the new information, excited by all they had witnessed, impressed by how much they had learned, and they were feeling proud to be a part of this opportunity. They were making new friends, too, as evidenced when they hugged one another goodbye. We would meet again in five months. They were to return to class with four new rug designs incorporating the design principles and finish the rug they'd started during this class, too.

With their tzutes tied and the women ready to depart, Reyna invited them to sit in a circle. She wanted to discuss her second announcement. She distributed a piece of paper and for those who could not read, she explained the contents and requested that they take it home to consider. Continuing, she said, "If you want to continue as a teacher in training, you must sign the document and bring it along when you attend the next session." The document spelled out our mutual

An Extraordinary Opportunity 47

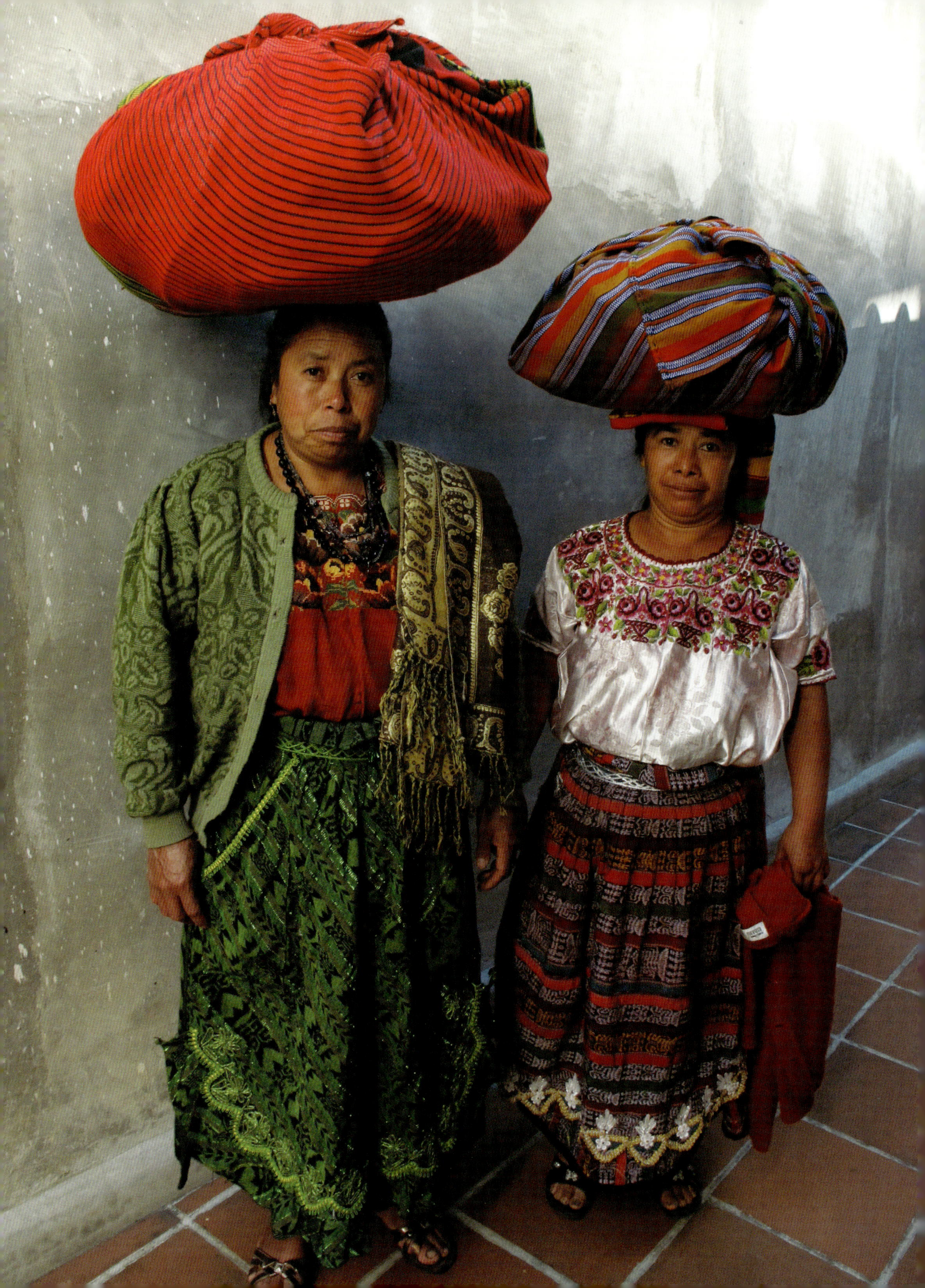

responsibilities—ours as workshop leaders—theirs as students. "By signing the document with your signature or thumbprint," she said, "you agree to work hard, to help one another, and to complete all the homework required in this class. You agree to attend each class and meetings in between classes, too. If you cannot agree to this, please do not waste our time or money. Because as you can see," she said, pointing to the class materials and to Jody and me, "it costs money to conduct this class. If you cannot fulfill your part, please let us know now because there are other women who would be happy to take your place." For our part as leaders, the document explained our pledge to help them succeed as rug-hooking teachers within their communities and to treat everyone with equal respect and consideration.

As the women picked up their tzutes and headed toward the door, I asked, "Any questions or comments about the homework?" No one spoke. I followed up with "Who is responsible for making sure you have everything you need to complete the homework?" I added, "If you are having trouble digesting all this information you must practice, practice, practice."

During later interviews with the artists, I asked Yolanda (who would later serve on Multicolores's board of directors) about her reaction to having to sign a contract to continue her participation in the project. My concern, in hindsight, focused on applying pressure to women whose lives were already pressured. I wondered how she felt about the contract.

Shrugging her shoulders, she replied, "It's okay to make participants sign because then everybody knows what is their responsibility. If they can't sign the document, maybe they shouldn't be in the program."

Reyna added, "If you offer skills, training, you want a sense of commitment to the project. This document was a way of creating commitment for our future success."

Jody, Reyna, and I decompressed after the workshop, discussing what lessons worked well, what lessons fell flat, who needed more help, and who seemed to excel. With the conviction of the newly converted, I remarked to Reyna that among the rug-hooking students, there sure seemed to be an unusual percentage of very talented women. But Reyna merely agreed with a resigned, "Yup." Her resignation resided in the frustratingly relentless fact that for an overwhelming number of Guatemala's women, access to opportunity is terribly remote. Reyna's truncated reply conveyed, "If only there were more opportunities, imagine what these women could accomplish."

OPPOSITE: Maria Sacalxot and Carmen, tzutes poised on their heads, prepare for their long journey home from teacher training.

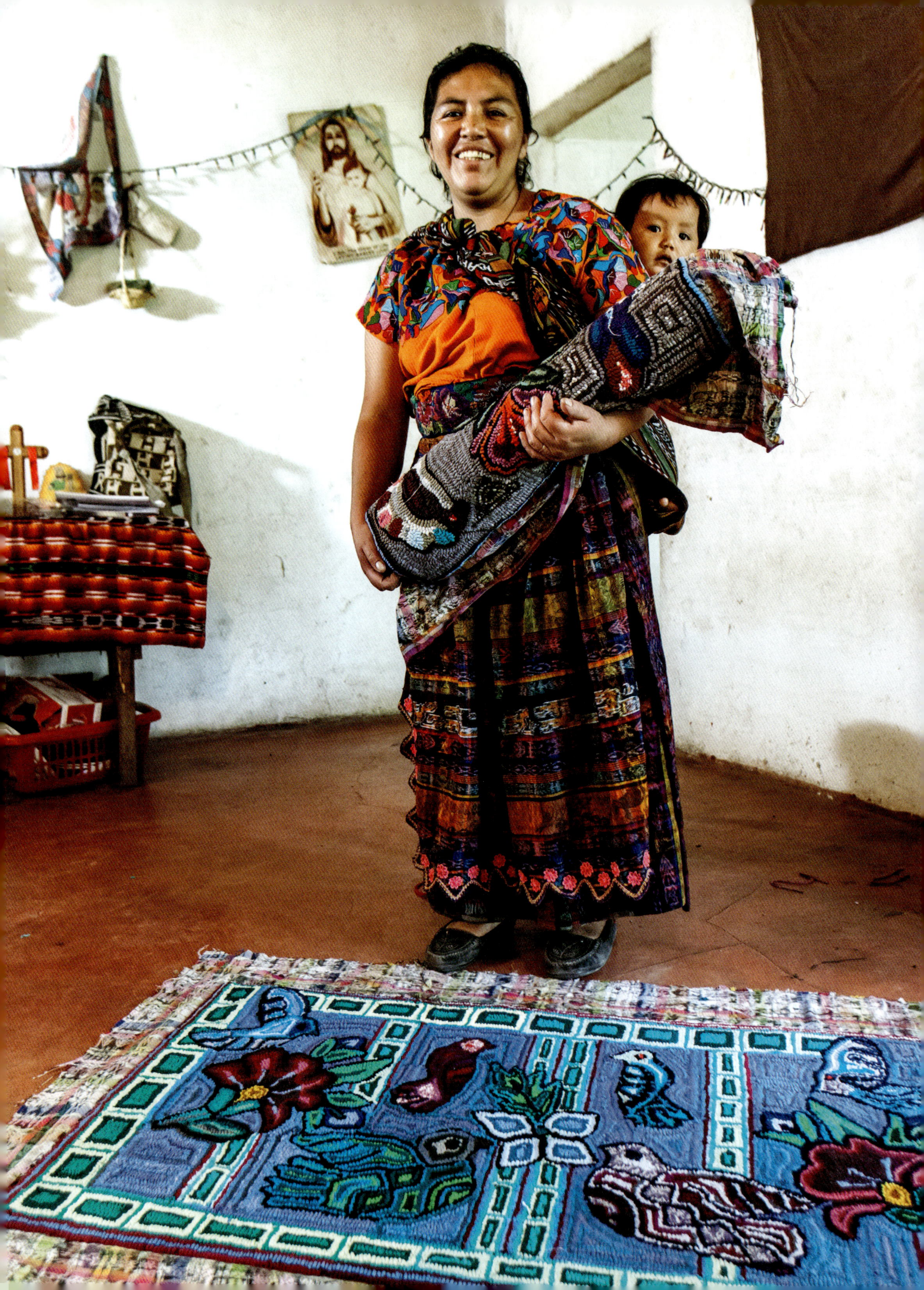

"By helping and respecting each other, we can all move forward together"
» Glendy Emiliana Muj Mendoza de Barreno, 33, Patanatic

Glendy is the calm and capable presence in the midst of chaos. Her training began as the eldest of ten children. At the age of eight, she was sent to babysit for a neighbor part time. The four dollars she earned a month didn't go far. There were many mouths to feed, and even as a young child, she realized that the herbs she collected in the mountains to extend the family's diet didn't go far enough. She knew the family needed more money for food. So Glendy dropped out of the fourth grade and took on a second job. She continued to babysit in the mornings and began working afternoons at a neighborhood *tienda* (store).

At age seventeen, she got married. Now in charge of her own household, Glendy determined that she would make a better life for her children.

Today, Glendy lives with her husband and seven children in Patanatic. To visit Glendy at her home is to test the endurance capacity of your knees: her house is perched on a steep mountainside slope and the approach is by foot, not by car. Arriving at her home, she invites you to climb a bit further to the rooftop where the splendor of Lake Atitlán sparkles in the distance. A lush canopy of trees provides shade for her neighborhood. Children's voices, busy at play, fill the air. The kids latch on to well-worn handholds and footholds, and undeterred by the steep slope, they swing from avocado trees to coffee bushes to orange trees in pursuit of their games. In spite of the fact that a misstep could result in serious injury, first-time visitors cannot help but envy the kids for growing up on this picturesque mountain.

Glendy started rug hooking in 2010. "Since I started rug hooking, our quality of life has greatly improved. Five of my children are in school; the eldest, now thirteen, wants to go to university. We are able to go to the doctor more frequently and buy medicine. With income from my first rug I bought a *pila* (outdoor sink), so now I can do the family's laundry at home, rather than carry heavy loads to the communal sink down the mountain." Fanning her apron to shoo a flock of baby chicks out of the house, Glendy continues. "We have made improvements to our home, we now have a concrete floor. I have a water pipe in our kitchen and our windows have glass; they are no longer open to the wind and the rain. We are also adding on to our home with a second level. We're able to do this because my income pays to sustain the house. My husband's income and a loan pay for the remodeling."

I asked Glendy to speak about her participation in Multicolores. *As members of Multicolores, we share the same philosophy, that by helping and respecting each other, we can all move forward together. No one is more important than another. This means that as a group, we are united and always mindful of others. I am teaching these values to my children, so that we can look to a future with more equality. My children see me as a role model; they see that without education and only a few opportunities, I have achieved much and have had many new experiences. This makes me happy*

Glendy Emiliana Muj Mendoza de Barreno

because they know that with an education, they will be able to reach further than I could. My children are contributing to our family's success, too. They have taken over many of my chores so I can do my rug-hooking work. It is good to see them become more responsible.

Glendy would like readers to know that the benefits of having mastered a craft go beyond her ability to buy things to improve her life. Through learning this skill, and growing their knowledge, she and her compañeras have become more confident.

I feel more comfortable talking in public—before being involved with this project, I was scared. The tours are one thing that have helped me overcome my shyness. And there have been changes in my family, too. When I go on the tour, I am away for several days at a time. I think back to when I participated on the first tour. Before I left for that first tour, I would make sure the house was tidy and I would prepare all the food for my family to eat while I was away from home. Now my husband tells me, "Don't worry, you go and have a good time. We will make the food." He trusts me, and I know my children will help him with the chores when I am away.

In speaking about her rug making, I asked Glendy, "What is your favorite part of the process?" She replied, "I like to draw, to imagine my designs, and then combine the colors. I don't like cutting the paca! So my husband helps me with that part of my work. Also, when I see others do good work, I am inspired to become better at rug making. Seeing good work motivates me."

The Second Teacher Training Class: Quality and Craftsmanship
» OB Sala, Panajachel, Guatemala, June 2012

At the start of the second teacher training session, we learned that Zoila hadn't signed the contract. Like many newlyweds, when Zoila married she moved into her husband's family household. As a new daughter-in-law, she was expected to help with domestic chores. But her husband had left for the United States to find work, and now Zoila and their infant son, Nestor, were left alone with her suegra. With her husband away and unable to defend her, Zoila's mother-in-law made her life miserable.

Zoila arrived at class with Nestor tied in a tzute on her back. A sense of sadness shadowed her. Her suegra, we learned, felt suspicious of Zoila's trips to Pana and certainly did not approve of her overnight absences. She wanted Zoila to stay home where she could keep tabs on her and have her help in managing the house. OB field workers had met the suegra and had tried to intervene, but she would not relent, refusing Zoila permission to sign the contract. Realizing the opportunity to participate in the teacher training classes could be taken away from her, Zoila felt increasingly despondent. Then one day, while on a FaceTime call with her husband, she held up a nearly completed rug for him to admire. He was impressed and encouraging and said he hadn't realized he'd married an artist. He gave his permission for her to continue with classes.

Two years later, we visited Zoila in the new house she shared with Nestor. Using money her husband sent home, along with her rug money, she built the house on a small plot of land away from her suegra. Marveling at her accomplishment, I wondered when her husband might return, and how one resumes a marriage after living apart for so many years.

Excited to see all the work completed since our first teacher training class, I announced a throw-down! Three of the women, Carmen, Zoila, and María, had sold their rugs after the last session but brought in a nearly completed second rug in addition to their design homework.

By now, the women were selling their rugs through special events and exhibits Jody and I coordinated in the U.S. OB sold rugs, too, in their tienda in Panajachel. Part of Reyna's job was to manage OB's tienda and stock it with products from various associations and with the hooked rugs, too. All rugs sold through OB's tienda were on consignment because OB did not have funds to buy them outright. But rugs Jody and I sold in the U.S. were paid for upon approval because by now, Reyna had a system of emailing us photos of rugs as they were delivered to the OB tienda. Via email, we'd make our selections, and the rugs we approved would be

Mary Anne works with Glendy on nuances of the color palette. OPPOSITE ABOVE: Mary Anne encourages the teachers-in-training to draw color and design inspiration from a variety of huipils. OPPOSITE BELOW: A rug hooked by Zoila illustrates quality and craftsmanship.

paid for on the spot through a fund we'd left with OB. Between OB and U.S. sales, some of the women had sold seven or eight rugs. The sales inspired the teachers and others to keep making rugs.

Privately, however, some of the women complained to Reyna that they didn't think it was fair to be paid the same price if their rugs were better crafted or included greater detail. We agreed. And so addressing this concern to the entire class and using the variety of rugs they'd just completed, Reyna directed them to examine the quality of craftsmanship. It was time to establish a mutually-agreed-upon quality ranking system.

She distributed scraps of paper written with the numerals 1, 2, and 3. She instructed the women to examine each rug and rank it according to the quality of the craftsmanship. Number 1 was the highest quality. They were to signify their opinion by placing the scrap of paper with the corresponding number onto each rug. Dropping to their knees, they crawled across the floor from one rug to the next and thoroughly and thoughtfully examined each rug. During a second round of critiquing, Reyna asked them to remark only on the design and to assign a rank to each rug.

An Extraordinary Opportunity 55

Gloria and Hilda from the Totonicapán rug-hooking group, share a light moment together. The Maya women cherish the friendships they form in the rug-hooking groups. BELOW: Carmen draws a design to transfer onto ground cloth. OPPOSITE: A vibrant rug exhibits mastery of the design principles.

Vocabulary from the critique session guided their exchange as they discussed how well a rug conformed to the design principles. In the end, only a few of the rugs had earned a #1 ranking in both craftsmanship and design.

Some of the women defended their own rugs and lobbied for higher rankings. Eventually, through quite a bit of discussion, the characteristics of a quality #1 standard were agreed upon. Rugs ranked #1 had designs that positively vibrated with energy and vitality; the rug lay flat, the nap height was consistent, and the edges of the rug did not curl under. All of these rugs were hooked with thinner strips of cloth and had greater detail. A rug of #2 quality was hooked with wider strips of cloth, the rug might not lay perfectly flat, and nap height was less consistent than for quality #1. The design might be very good, even quality #1, but the craftsmanship would lower the ranking. A quality #3 rug had the least detail because it was hooked with wider strips. The design might be good, but the edges likely curled under, the nap height was inconsistent, and the surface might contain fraying strips.

Having reached a consensus on the criteria for each ranking, Reyna then asked the group's opinion about the prices paid according to the rank. Everyone agreed that a well-crafted rug with a good design should command a higher price, and payments were adjusted to reflect the new quality ranking system. Overnight, or so it seemed, the quality of their craftsmanship improved.

Later, I asked Yolanda about her pricing concerns. She said, "Yes, this was my complaint. I felt hurt knowing that others were getting paid the same amount of money for lesser quality. It made me wonder why I was working so hard. But I talked to Reyna about it, and then she adjusted prices paid according to the quality. I knew my rugs would always sell first because of the high quality and it was very important then, and it's still important now, to be paid when I deliver my rug. It's one of the most important things about this project, to be paid right away and not wait for things to sell on consignment."

Turning back to the rugs, I spied several whose ranking might improve with a little reworking. "Time for an impromptu object lesson," I thought. First asking the artist's permission, I chose a few rugs to pin to the wall. I said, "This is a practice used by artists the world over. You can do this in your homes, too. This practice will help you see your work from a different perspective." Then I proceeded to cut snippets of cloth from scraps in confetti-sized pieces using a variety of colors. As I positioned the bits of scraps onto each rug, as if the rug were a felt storyboard, I asked them to observe the simple changes to the design, if any. To a dull gray field, I added contrasting bits of colored fabric. Several of them gasped because the design came to life. Hearing their reaction, I asked, "Did you feel the difference in your body?" Then Ramona T. produced a rug, pinned it to the wall and said she was unsure about the choice of the border color. She wondered if I had a suggestion. Pulling several colors from the paca pile, I tore long strips of cloth the width and length of her border, laying various options on top of her hooking until she could "see" and "feel" a better choice.

From this point forward, when someone wanted to know what I thought about the use of a particular color, I responded, "What am I going to suggest you do?" Invariably, she would cut strips of cloth to answer her question.

That afternoon, we introduced colored pencils. None of the women, except Yolanda, in her training with Maya Traditions, had worked with colored pencils. The women quickly understood the value of designing with color. They practiced working the lead, experimenting with pressing hard to achieve a saturated color, using a softer touch for a lighter shade, and laying one color on top of another to form a blend.

Several years later, I asked Glendy if she was still using colored pencils to design rugs. "The teacher training class was the first time I'd worked with colored pencils. I don't need them now because I can envision what colors I need, and besides, the colors of the pencils are not the same colors as my paca fabrics."

The six days of workshop concluded with an explanation of the homework assignment—more designs, more finished rugs—and the announcement that Reyna would hold a class session before Jody and I returned. The point of the interim class, she said, was to see how well they were implementing their designs and troubleshoot any problems.

But just as they began to pack up their materials, Carmen had a problem to discuss. She was halfway through her rug when she ran out of her field color. She went to several pacas and couldn't find a similar color, nothing even close. She wondered what she should do. I sat with Carmen on the floor and asked her to take a string and lay it on top of her rug as if she were dividing her rug in half. Turning to the others, I asked, "Have any of you had this running-out-of-materials problem?" Yes, they all had experienced this, but most had succeeded in finding the right color or a color close enough. I suggested, "To avoid this in the future, before you begin your rug, divide your field colors and place them in two equal piles. Put one pile in a bag and set it aside. If you have to reach into that bag for colors before you are halfway through your rug, you will know to make some adjustments in your plan."

Carmen considered this for only a moment and then reached for a second string to now divide her rug into quarter sections. She said, "Yes, I could even divide my first half of the pile into two piles and if I have to use the second bag from my first half, I'd know if I was going to run out even quicker." I threw her a wide smile for she instantly had comprehended my meaning—and took it one step further. Hers was a better plan.

Yolanda and Estela evaluate color and design while Reyna looks on. OPPOSITE: A rug hooked by Micaela shows an understanding of balance and strong sense of color.

58   An Extraordinary Opportunity

Reyna then suggested, "Now that you are all earning money with your rugs, maybe you should begin to lay up a stash of paca clothing." All at once they all started to talk about their paca shopping experiences. María Sacalxot explained that neighbors stop by once or twice a month to sell her their used clothes and that never happened before rug hooking. Rosmery told of an arrangement she'd made with her local paca vendor who, once a month, burns all the old clothes he can't sell. "Now before he burns his piles he calls me." With a proud smile of accomplishment, she continued, "He sells me paca at really, really good prices." Ramona T. said she had been embarrassed to go into the pacas and felt shy to shop in them. "Before rug hooking, I would shop at pacas once in a while, but I would only buy things that were hanging up, easy to see, things like a sweater for me. But when I needed paca for my rugs, it was more economical to buy the biggest pieces I could find and that meant I had to dig deep into the piles to find those big pieces. I felt embarrassed to be buying such huge clothes because the paca workers would ask, 'Who are you buying such big pieces for?' Now I don't care anymore." Now she's developed favorite paca stores and knows when they put things on sale and that is when she buys.

Before the third and final teacher training class, Ramona T. phoned Reyna to say she was dropping out. She'd learned that she was pregnant and her husband did not support her traveling back and forth to class. He had recently returned to Guatemala from the United States where he had labored for nine years. During this time, he didn't dare return to Guatemala to visit Ramona for fear he would be unable to make his way back to the U.S. Now safely returned to Guatemala for good, he worried that Ramona's three-and-a-half-hour journey to class might harm their baby.

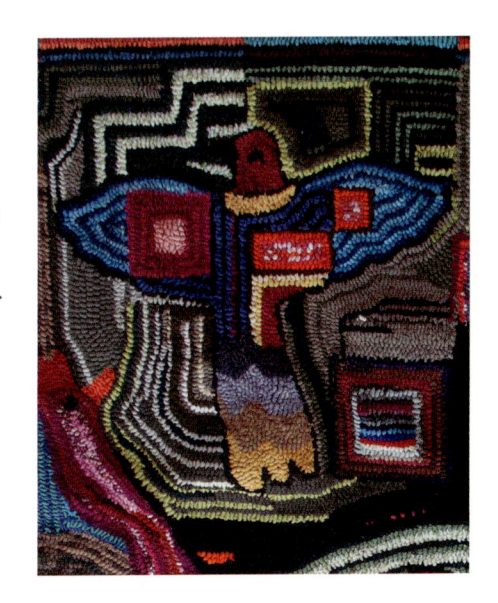

An Extraordinary Opportunity

Reyna Teaches Solo: Leadership and Commitment
» OB Sala, Panajachel, Guatemala, August 2012

The point of the teachers' meeting between training sessions was to further coalesce as a team and to establish Reyna in the position as the project's coleader. OB's director Ramona recognized that Jody and I could not direct the project's growth from Wisconsin and, during the workshops, she observed Reyna's leadership skills over and over again. These qualities, along with our easy rapport and Reyna's command of English, made her the obvious choice to become the project's coleader. In addition, she had an uncanny ability to "read" people's intentions and had garnered the women's trust and respect because she was evenhanded and approachable. Jody and I welcomed the news of Reyna's ascension as coleader. Over the course of the teacher training, she had become the cultural barometer from which key decisions were made, decisions that were beyond Jody's and my capacity as extranjeras to fully comprehend. Not insignificantly, Reyna made me a better teacher. She helped reorganize the sequence of my lesson plans to successfully build upon the women's knowledge and experiences, brick by brick. She also knew when to push them harder—and when to pull back.

Reyna had a lot to accomplish during this daylong teachers' meeting. The new teachers would each soon recruit a new student, and Reyna wanted to discuss the personal characteristics of the prospective recruits. Her interest in carefully choosing new students was piqued in response to an eruption of *chisme* (gossip) in one of the rug-hooking groups. Going forward, she wanted to create a community of motivated rug-hooking participants within a culture dedicated to equality among peers and a shared sense of responsibilities, including leadership. Reyna knew that self-anointed leaders, unwilling to share control, characterized groups plagued by chisme. Thinking ahead to the selection of new recruits, Reyna wanted to nip chisme in the bud.

60   An Extraordinary Opportunity

Reflecting back on that time, Reyna described how she dealt with the issue. When visiting each community, she gathered the group together and encouraged them to solve their problems as a group. She told them, "If you come to me with a problem in private, you had better have spoken about the issue to your group because when I visit, I will talk about the problem in front of everyone, and I will ask you to explain why you told me the problem." The women quickly learned to deal with their issues within the group.

Carmen's Chirijquiac group had just completed ten rugs prior to the teachers' meeting, so Carmen brought them with her. The variety of these rugs provided Reyna an impromptu opportunity to observe the teachers as they conducted an evaluation, ranking the rugs' quality #1, #2, or #3. Reyna determined that their evaluations were consistent, which meant they were able to perceive the difference in quality. The importance of the ranking system was significant because Cultural Cloth had just opened a store in Wisconsin and pledged to buy any rug with a quality #1 ranking. The women would earn more money with a quality #1 rug. Not only that, if the rug was judged quality #1, the woman would be paid on the spot. There was no waiting for a rug to sell on consignment at OB.

Reyna is committed to creating a culture of equality and shared responsibility for all the rug-hooking group leaders. OPPOSITE: Colors radiate from intricate, perfectly placed designs in Zoila's exquisite rug.

This news meant more control over their income. If school was starting, for example, and money was needed to buy schoolbooks for their kids, the women could anticipate the expenditure and plan their production time accordingly. If a woman had dreams of home repairs, such as bringing a water pipe into her home to plumb her kitchen, she could schedule her production time. Knowing she would be paid upon delivery for a quality #1 rug, she could budget and save money. For some, a measure of stress had been eased. For others, the motivation to improve their quality, and receive a higher price, had increased.

The rug hookers often took turns delivering their group's rugs to Pana. Sometimes a woman arrived at the office with seven or eight quality #1 rugs and she would be paid on the spot. She returned home carrying a large sum of money. I knew that many of their homes were situated in remote locations off the main road, and I wondered if they were concerned about traveling back home with so much money. "Our husbands now accompany us from the highway to home. Sometimes they even meet us at a closer location!" And one woman added, "My husband would like to learn to hook rugs, too."

During a break, Yolanda told Reyna she had an upcoming opportunity to teach weaving to a norteamericana. The problem, she explained, was the timing. Her opportunity coincided with the next teacher training class that Jody and I would

An Extraordinary Opportunity   61

be giving. The teaching money was good, and therefore she would not be present for the first two days of the next class. Disappointed, because Yolanda had signed the contract defining her responsibilities, Reyna listened to this news without comment.

The teacher training program began with ten women but shortly after the first session, we asked one woman, Delores, to withdraw. She was very active in her community and her obligations caused her to miss a mandatory teachers' meeting. Her responsibilities as a teacher-in-training included attending all classes and were defined in the contract she had signed. In addition, Delores was three months late in delivering a commission, a deadline she'd agreed to when she accepted the work. Reyna understood that Delores's priorities would likely not change, and she did not want to invest more resources in training a woman unable to fully participate. She worried, too, that Delores's behavior would have a dispiriting effect upon the remaining students. So we asked Delores to leave the program, which she did, reluctantly. With Delores's recent departure in mind, and now Yolanda's announcement that she would miss half of the upcoming session, Reyna decided it was time for another evaluation.

Reyna distributed pieces of red, green, and yellow colored paper to each woman. "Just as you ranked rugs," she said, "I would like you to rank your participation in this class so far. Listen to each question and grade yourself by holding up the green paper for 'really good,' or the yellow paper for 'okay, but needs improvement,' or the red paper for 'not good.'" She did not mention Delores's departure from the program because her empty chair was evidence. Reyna asked, "Do you value this opportunity?" All held up the green paper. "Do you think it will help you earn more money?" All held up the green paper. "How well have you complied with homework assignments?" All held up the green paper. "How well do you share the information learned in class with your compañeras back home?" Their responses were divided between those holding green and yellow papers. "Do you think the teacher training will lead to additional opportunities for you and your group?" All held up the green paper.

Yessika selects the appropriate colors for the border of a new rug design. OPPOSITE: In Silvia Ajcot's gorgeous rug, the dynamic border frames two birds, a classic motif in textile designs of the Lake Atitlán region.

After class, Yolanda pulled Reyna aside and said, "I understand my responsibility is with my compañeras in this class. I will attend all days of the next training session."

After learning about this red, yellow, and green self-judging exchange, I asked Reyna, "What made you think of this exercise where you ask people to vote about their participation?"

"It was a way to quickly cut through, to declare publicly how they believe, how they feel about this opportunity. Even if they don't really feel that way, they have declared themselves in front of their compañeras. So then I know their public position, I know how they feel, and I can ask them what is happening if they don't follow through. I can hold them accountable because of how they voted. It's about taking this opportunity seriously."

Less than one year later, with more women coming into the program and Jody's and my visits less frequent and with Reyna busy managing the project, Yolanda was selected as the "roving rug-hooking ambassador." It was her job to travel once a month to each of the five rug-hooking communities scattered across the highlands and check on production. During her visits, she helped troubleshoot and checked on quality control or suggested design revisions. She knew that none of the women could afford to hook a rug that wouldn't sell. In front of each group, she would subtly assert her fellow teacher's position as leader in the community, teachers like Rosmery in Totonicapán and Glendy in Patanatic. But her most significant role was to motivate women who felt discouraged by their lack of progress. She would say, "I know how you feel; I would often get discouraged, too. But look at me. I never thought I would be hired to do a job like this, not in my wildest dreams, because after all, I only went to the sixth grade. But I stuck with this technique even when I felt like quitting, and do you know what? If I can do this—I know you can, too." Then, reaching for her hook and placing the problem rug onto her lap, she would say, "Here, let me help you."

On reflecting upon her experiences as roving rug-hooking ambassador, Yolanda said, "I basically tried to encourage the women. I know what it's like to not have money or work and to feel frustrated when you can't do something. And I know this job was an opportunity for me to give something back for all the opportunities I've been given. It is an honor to help my compañeras succeed."

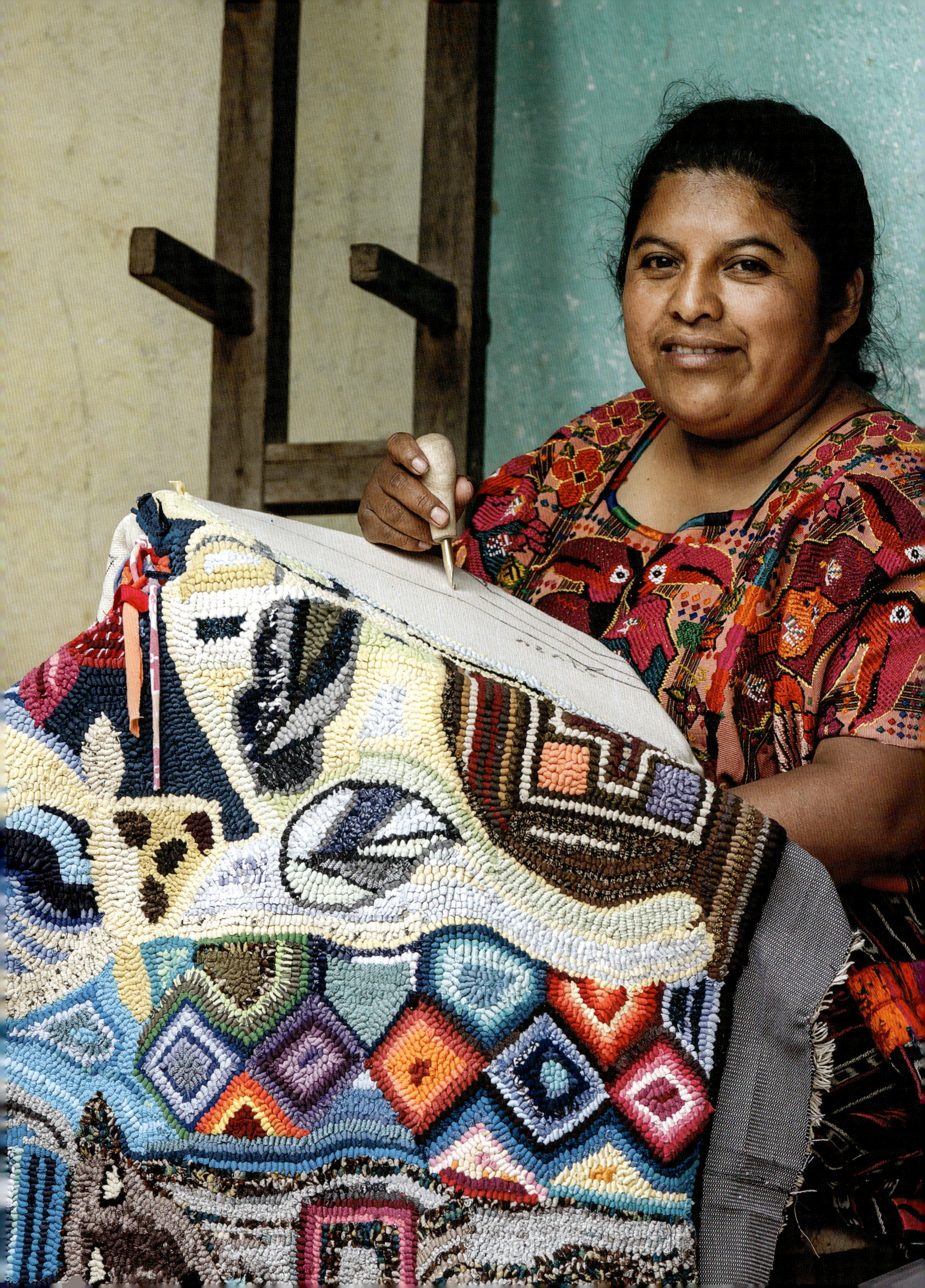

"The rug is like a canvas"
» Yolanda Sebastiana Calgua de Sucunu, 37, Quiejel

Yolanda left school at the sixth grade to help support her family, but lack of formal education could not suppress her entrepreneurial instincts. People are attracted to Yolanda. And if you display the slightest hint of promise, or even interest, she will quickly incorporate you into her ever-growing circle of opportunities. Yolanda is a force of nature.

Her husband, Esteban, a carpenter, built the comfortable compound they share with their two teenage children. Their home, near Chichicastenango, has a peaceful view of the highlands with mountains that recede into the distance as far as the eye can see. They grow vegetables and raise chickens, turkeys, and pigs, and she sells some of their produce at the local farmer's market. Her mother and other family members live close by, a hilly footpath away.

Yolanda learned how to weave from her mother and grandmother. She still weaves most of her clothing on one of her three backstrap looms. She is proud of her weaving proficiency. But her drive to expand her textile repertoire, and her options to earn income, led her to participate in the first rug-hooking workshop in 2009. She remembers the rug she designed for that workshop, made in honor of her grandmother. The rug incorporated designs from her grandmother's huipil, a cherished family heirloom that had been passed down to her.

Recalling the first rug-hooking class, she is now able to laugh at the memory because "the quality of my rug was not good. Esteban wondered who would buy the rugs, and listening to his worry caused my morale to be down. I started to think I was not capable, but that changed as, little by little, we learned more about quality and good designs and we all improved.
I remember the design principles in the teacher training class. That was good to learn. I still use those principles; in fact, they are useful for many areas of my craft work."

In addition to participating on Multicolores's board of directors, Yolanda is a valued member of Maya Traditions; she and her group produce backstrap weaving to specifications. She's become a borrower at Friendship Bridge, a microlending organization through which she has garnered attention

Yoland Sebastiana Calgua de Sucunu

66 Yoland Sebastiana Calgua de Sucunu

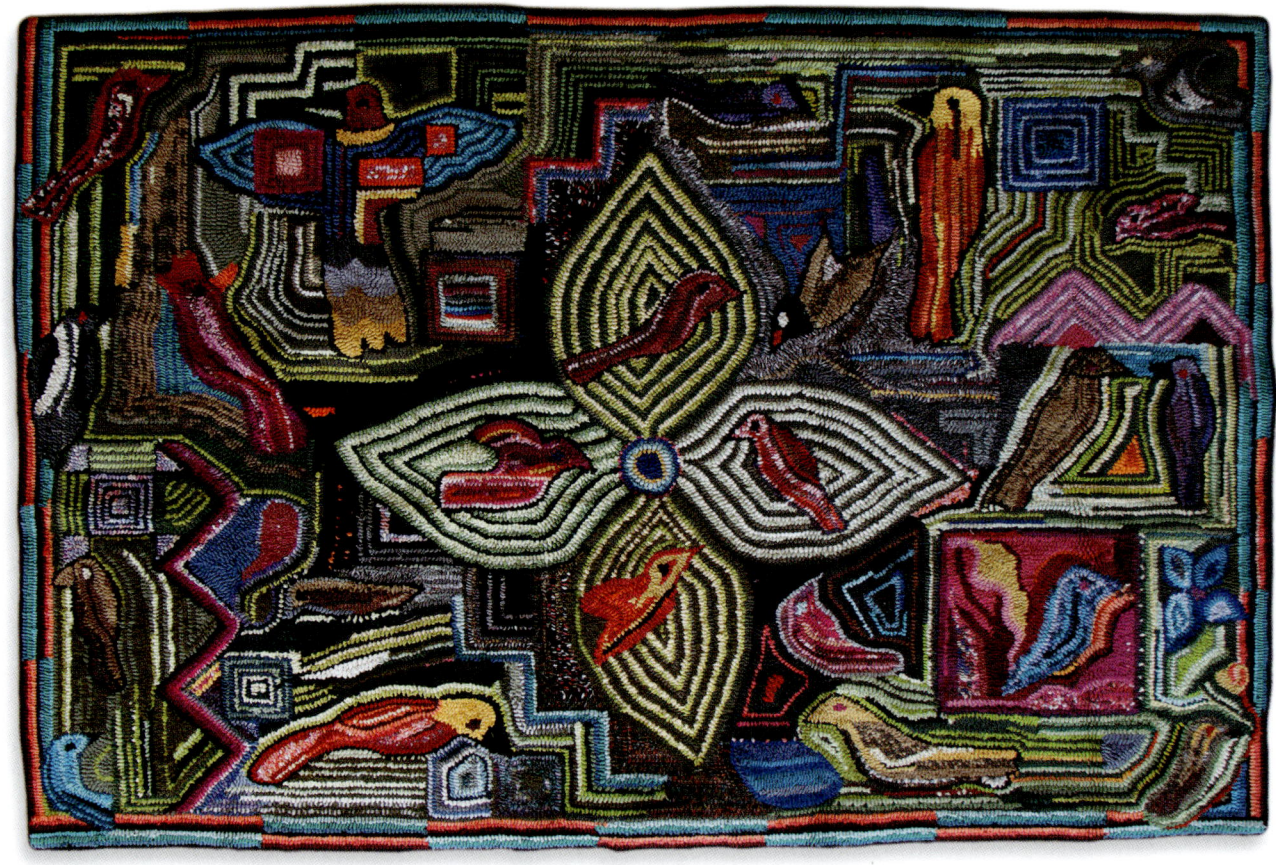

for her entrepreneurial talents. In addition, she recently participated in a craft development project for AGEXPORT, a national organization that sources Guatemalan handcrafts to global markets. Participating in these activities helps her grow her network and learn new things. In discussing all the areas of her involvement, she shakes her head, "I sometimes find it difficult to juggle all these opportunities!" Her comments remind me of busy women everywhere who overextend themselves as they reach for new challenges.

In 2017, Esteban completed a new workshop building for Yolanda and her compañeras. As further evidence of her industry, the new workshop includes a small tienda where she sells handcrafts produced by her group, including weaving and embroidery. That Yolanda has a tienda, and that her home is only accessible via a long, remote footpath twenty minutes off the paved highway, speaks to the volume of visitors and her abilities to attract them.

Yolanda is quick to credit Multicolores with the opportunities she enjoys today. "You believed in me, and through Multicolores I realized many goals, such as traveling to Los Estados Unidos, not once, not twice, but three times! I have met many people through my work with Multicolores, and I have been able to enjoy new opportunities through those contacts."

As a rug-hooking teacher in her community and also a former roving rug-hooking ambassador for Multicolores, Yolanda helped others succeed at the craft. Helping women like María Ignacia (see page 118) succeed, earn money, and change their self-perception has been a rewarding experience. She strongly believes in the power of women to bring about positive social change in Guatemala because she has seen the change in herself. "Doing this work for Multicolores has given me recognition, and I am grateful for the opportunity to help my compañeras succeed. Because I am so busy, my husband now helps me at my rug hooking. It's become a joint effort, we both work on the designs, the colors, cutting the paca. He enjoys it, and I enjoy working with him. There are many events in my life that I am able to incorporate into my rugs. The rug is like a canvas that I fill with the colors, symbols, and designs that represent Guatemala. Sometimes I have so many ideas for rugs I can't sleep."

The Third Teacher Training: Through the Looking Glass
» OB Sala, Panajachel, Guatemala, October 2012

On the first day of our third teacher training session, we were surprised to see seventeen-year-old Rosmery arrive at class on time. She looked as fresh and bright-eyed as ever. Our surprise was in knowing that two days before class, there had been a demonstration in her village and several people had been killed—the incident was widely reported in the newspapers. In the wake of the unrest, the village lay tense. No one expected young Rosmery to navigate her way to the bus stop undaunted amidst the protestors. As she entered the sala, Reyna exclaimed, "Rosmery! How are you! We didn't think we'd see you!"

Unfazed, Rosmery replied, "If it came to it, I would've crawled on my knees to get here."

Marta, Rosmery's twenty-eight-year-old colleague from the same village, opted not to attend this teacher training session, citing the village unrest as the reason she stayed home. Her decision prompted the OB staff to meet and discuss the situation. That young Rosmery found the courage and motivation to attend the session and Marta did not resulted in the decision to dismiss Marta from the program. The teacher training program was now down to seven participants.

Settling down to work, I was pleased to note that each woman was seated next to a classmate other than her village mate. This seemingly insignificant gesture signaled a subtle shift, as if they accepted and were growing into their roles as teachers. The gesture was not lost on Jody, Reyna, or me.

Today's lesson was about symmetrical and asymmetrical designs and the concept of balance. Symmetrical designs were increasingly showing up in their rugs. I didn't want them to rely on formulaic design decisions, and I worried that if they relied upon symmetry, their progress as artists could devolve. I wanted them to understand the concept of balance versus symmetry. Balance, I believed, held greater artistic potential than a symmetrical design.

By now, everyone had pulled out their homework consisting of small rug drawings, and they were touching them up with their colored pencils. They continued drawing as I attempted to explain balance, symmetry, and asymmetry. "You can start out with a symmetrical design but exaggerate the scale of at least some of the elements within the drawing to achieve balance, not symmetry. If you do this, you'll likely end up with a design that possesses energy, vitality, and an essential life force. You know," I said, pointing to the design principle icons taped to the wall, "like design principle #5?"

Courageous and committed, Rosmery understands the value of her participation in the rug-hooking project.

My explanation of symmetry bore on and on. One look at Reyna confirmed what I knew—I'd lost them. I searched my mind, wondering how to win them back right now. And then I remembered using mirrors to communicate design intent during my early days as a rug weaver in the days before computer-aided design. When presenting rug drawings to a client for approval, rather than painstakingly drawing the entire rug, if I used a mirror I could get away with drawing only half the woven rug. Positioning a pocket mirror upright on the edge of the page facing your drawing, you can look into the mirror and "see" the entire drawing. This method of communicating design intent was common in the carpet showrooms that once represented Jody's and my woven rugs. It's where I learned the trick.

Pulling Jody aside, I told her my idea to communicate symmetry. She remembered the mirror trick, too. Flagging down a tuk-tuk, she raced to the market and bought small pocket mirrors.

The response to our mirror demonstration was instantaneous—the room exploded with delight. The women looked into the mirrors with surprise and awe as a kaleidoscope of options magically appeared in the glass, as if a miniature planet had suddenly been born on the page before them. Carmen maneuvered her mirrors with a sense of wonder as design possibilities were revealed one after another. Pausing only a moment, she threw me a look that said, "So! This is symmetry!" She placed a second mirror at ninety degrees to her first mirror and in the corner where her mirrors met, she saw a world of more options. Narrowing the angle, she looked into the mirror and saw more options yet. Working alongside her, Rosmery squealed with surprise. Across the room, I noticed Zoila had already mastered the mirrors, using them like chopsticks to pick up her paper and position, then reposition, and position again. Watching her absorb the possibilities, I knew Zoila would bank them all.

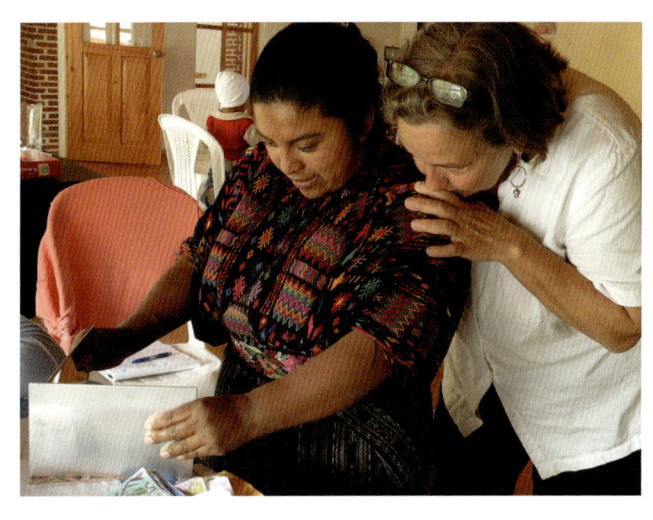

Using mirrors, Mary Anne helps the artists to understand concepts of symmetry and balance, offering yet another layer of possibility for their designs.

The homework assignment was to use the mirrors to create more designs and this time, to exaggerate a portion of the drawing so it was not symmetrical. Everyone understood.

The next morning, we got right to work. By now the process had become familiar: enlarge the scale of your small design onto paper the same size as your finished rug. "What do artists the world over call this full-sized drawing?" I asked.

"*Dibujo a escala*," they replied, ("Drawing at scale.") I watched them work as they adjusted their full-scale drawings to add more detail here or remove an element there. "The large paper pattern can be used for what?" I asked.

An Extraordinary Opportunity

Replying dully in unison, because by now my frequent reminders had begun to wear thin, they nonetheless complied and said, "For-a-second-rug-at-a-later-date."

As we worked throughout the morning, cell phone after cell phone rang, interrupting the work flow. Student after student darted out of the classroom to speak privately to her caller. Reyna reminded them, "Your cell phones are supposed to be turned off during class—please do that now." And then two more cell phones rang. Frustrated, Reyna grabbed a basket and holding it before each student, she collected their phones. In response to Reyna's demand, they looked at her as if she had a machete and was about to chop off their hands. They groaned and feigned hugging their phones because their phones are, indeed, their lifelines. Reyna and I exchanged satisfied looks and started to return to work when another cell phone rang. The ring tone was emanating from my pocket. The offending phone was mine! Everyone roared with laughter and pointed fingers at me and, with guilt written across my face, I reached for the basket.

With the afternoon winding down and the women anticipating their long journey home, they stood, stretching tired muscles, and slowly packed their tzutes. Watching as they packed, Jody and I engaged them in conversation. By now, all of them had been earning money through rug hooking for well over a year. Indeed, Reyna had begun to track their production and knew, for example, that Zoila and Carmen were the top two producers. It was also noted that neither had husbands at home, a fact none of us thought coincidental. We were simply curious to know how they spent their rug money. Anticipating their answers, we imagined they were able to buy more food, or perhaps they could better afford medicine or school supplies for their children.

Instead, and taken unaware, we heard stories that riveted us to the spot.

Yolanda told of a recent potable water project in her village. A special faucet was required to tap into the pipe to access the water. "The faucet was too expensive, and none of my neighbors could afford it. But I saved my rug money, and I bought six faucets for six families including my own family." As she explained her rationale for these purchases, she grew emotional and held us in her gaze.

Carmen spoke next. In a voice made sober by the memory, she said, "Before these classes, I believed I was nothing. I was a low person. I believed that because I don't read, I can't write, and I don't speak much Spanish. But now that I am selling my rugs, I have a different opinion of myself. I see the world differently, and I am happy because I never thought that would be possible. I am not a low person anymore."

Carmen may be the class clown, but she also has moments of quiet reflection as she expresses the value of Multicolores in her life. OPPOSITE: A beautiful rug hooked by Carmen Cua from the Chirijquiac group illustrates the value of a neutral background to bring out the richness of the design colors.

Graduation!
» OB Sala, Panajachel, Guatemala, October 29, 2012

Entering the sala we quickly greeted one another and went right to work. Excitement permeated the air because our graduation ceremony would take place today. No one needed any instruction because all knew what to do. Untying their tzutes, they removed their newly finished rugs for the throw-down. First, they placed their rugs around the room's perimeter and then they filled the room's interior. There were so many new works, they filled the floor! Walking amidst the colorful mosaic of carpets, the women studied one another's work and silently calculated each rug's ranking. Scanning the rugs with a sense of admiration, I observed that in the span of two years some of the women had attained a recognizable style, something any artist would envy. And then I watched the teachers break into pairs and critique the rugs using their new vocabulary and methods learned in class.

Excitement continued to build as the familiar voices of OB field workers drifted into the open windows from the garden below. They had begun preparations for the afternoon's graduation ceremony. We heard Andres the *guardián* (groundskeeper) tell a joke as he arranged the chairs in rows under the two tents erected to shade our guests. Nancy, OB's accomplished office manager, laughed a response while adding finishing touches to the mortarboards she'd fashioned from black construction paper. Balloons festooned the tent poles and crepe-paper streamers adorned the stage. A celebratory mood was in the air. Our focus was not on rug making—today was a day to enjoy our collective accomplishments.

The teachers' new students would arrive the next day, women they had recruited from their villages. Reyna and I would observe their class. In preparation for the class, the teachers and Reyna were meeting to divvy assignments and decide who would cover each topic on the curriculum and how the curriculum should flow. Working as a team, the teachers got busy cutting ground cloth for their students' first rugs, organizing stacks of paper and pencils, and hanging huipils on the wall for design inspiration.

While the teachers met with Reyna to plan for the next crop of rug-hooking students, I met with Ramona and Cheryl Conway, OB's development director. We met to lay the groundwork for the future of the project. Cheryl had joined OB ten months earlier. She spoke fluent Spanish and would occasionally assist in the classroom to help with translations. She had a respectful and warm rapport with the women, a feeling, I noted, the women returned. Behind the scenes, she also wrote grants, drew budgets, corresponded with funders and collected empirical data. Along with Reyna, she knew who were the top rug producers and who was having production problems and the reasons behind the problems, too. Perhaps a child had a prolonged illness or maybe a husband had started drinking, again. Both Cheryl and Reyna understood the impact of the program upon the rug hookers' lives.

An Extraordinary Opportunity

María Sacalxot pulls paca through ground cloth.

Ramona had recently announced her resignation from OB, and, in the wake of her announcement, she, Cheryl, Reyna, Jody, and I had begun a conversation about a new direction for our project. As OB transitioned without Ramona and as the rug-hooking project grew, we agreed that a legal, independent nonprofit would best fulfill the project's needs. Cheryl and Reyna would also transition from OB to devote themselves solely to the rug-hooking project. We needed to work out many details, but we all agreed upon the proposed organizational structure. Several months later, Cheryl, Reyna, Jody, and I established the rug-hooking project as an independent Guatemalan-based nonprofit. In March of 2014, we met with a lawyer to finalize the legal paperwork. By unanimous consent, Reyna became the president. I became the vice president, Glendy the secretary, Yolanda the treasurer, Ramona Kirschenman, the vocal. Jody and Cheryl were part of the general assembly. The rug hookers were our charter members, but what if one day our organization were to embrace craft categories other than rug hooking? What should we call ourselves? Glendy suggested Multicolores (Many Colors) and the name stuck.

After that pivotal first meeting with Ramona and Cheryl, I returned to the preparations for the graduation ceremony. I walked into the classroom now transformed as a changing room. The women had donned their ceremonial huipils and sat placidly braiding one another's hair. I immediately noted that the action of combing and braiding hair had the effect of calming nerves jangled in anticipation of the upcoming festivities. Reyna stood in their midst, holding bobby pins in her mouth. Having distributed gifts of combs and barrettes, she was now busy braiding long strands of dark hair. The scene was intensely feminine. Her obvious tenderness toward the women caused a lump to catch in my throat. She understood that the single photo from today would be hung in a prominent place in each of their homes, and she knew they wanted to look their best.

I peeked out the window to the garden below and saw that María Sacalxot's husband and granddaughter were the first to arrive. He politely removed his hat and, holding his granddaughter's hand, took a seat in the second row. More family members arrived. The event was getting underway. Yolanda's mother, husband, daughter, and son had taken seats, positioning themselves close to the front. Sindy's suegra arrived accompanied by Glendy's suegra and her sister-in-law, too. Zoila's suegra did not attend, but I felt happy for Rosmery, noting that her mother had arrived. Rosmery's mother, I knew, was a hard woman who had not supported her daughter's participation in the training. She did not support Rosmery's participation, that is, until Rosmery's rugs began to sell and Rosmery began to bring rug money home. Her presence would mean a lot to Rosmery. There were other guests, too, including Margaret Blood, founder of Mil Milagros, a local NGO. Margaret helped with the translations during the ceremony. I was pleased to see Ling Tan, owner of Chinitas restaurant on Santander, in the audience. Ling served on OB's board of directors.

Ramona K. made congratulatory remarks and reflected upon the rug hookers' extraordinary accomplishments. One by one, the women lined up and were called to the stage to receive their diplomas. We hugged one another as they wiped away tears, standing shoulder to shoulder across the stage to face the audience and to accept their applause. María, the oldest of the graduates, a woman who had attended school through the third grade, sobbed into my sleeve and confessed, "I am fifty years old—I never thought I'd see the day when I received a diploma."

Before arriving in Guatemala, Cheryl had been a researcher at Queen's University in Belfast, Northern Ireland, then Durham University and Newcastle University, both in the north of England. Her academic career spanned eighteen years with a research focus on economic development as well as gender and development. Her desire to leave academia was fueled by an interest in international development. She arrived in Guatemala in pursuit of this interest. Cheryl came to believe that the rug-hooking project, in particular, had benefits she'd not observed in other programs. She attributes this to the constancy of "the team"—Reyna, Jody, her, and me—who have been with the project since the beginning and who have created a supportive and trusting environment within which the women can grow and distinguish themselves as individuals. Through the project's innovative approach, she began to observe a real change. As the women mastered the technique and earned income, they appeared more self-confident, as if they had found their voice. As the project continued, it became clear to Cheryl that the women saw real possibilities for change because their life choices had expanded. Poverty was no longer a common thread that was expected to run from one generation to the next.

Cheryl's commitment to the women and her dedication to the project would soon keep the program afloat during 2013, the year the project transitioned out of OB and into our new nonprofit organization where the project, and the artists, would enjoy more autonomy. During this transitional period, Cheryl worked for an entire year without a salary.

An Extraordinary Opportunity

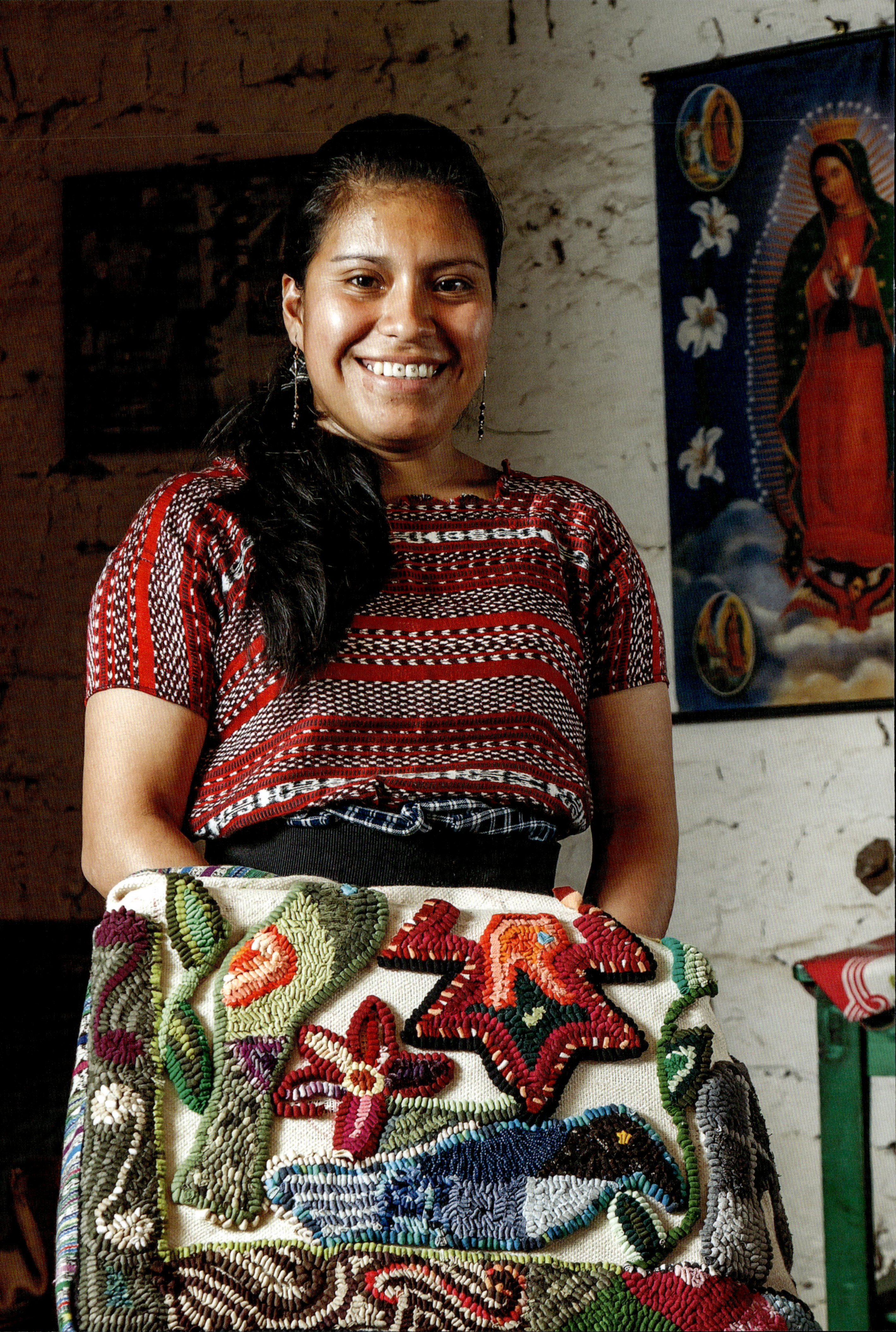

"Every rug is part of my story"
» Rosmery Elizabeth Pacheco, 21, Totonicapán

In preparing for this book, I sat down with Rosmery to discuss her artistry, her life, and her dreams. I've known and admired this determined and talented young woman for seven years. We enjoy a warm rapport. I opened the conversation by asking, "What would you like our readers to know about you?" Without pausing to gather her thoughts, she replied as if the answer was ever present in her mind. "There are two Rosmerys. The one before the rug-hooking project was timid and lived in a dark box. That is how I thought of my life, that is all I thought my life would be. I didn't know anything else. I thought I would always accompany my mother to clean houses. But through this project, I have learned so many things; you are looking at a different Rosmery now. The world has many more possibilities."

Continuing, she added, "The opportunities I have been given through Multicolores, there are so many. They believe in me, and the opportunities have helped me grow. They have not abandoned me. Through these experiences I have become a more confident person." Pantomiming holding a key and turning it, she added, "When I joined the project, I saw how others were growing skills. I could see how they were unlocking their world. I wasn't sure I could learn those skills and unlock my world, but I did. And now my mind is open to so much more. I have capabilities I don't even know about. I want to learn more. I want to travel and accomplish many things."

Rosmery lives in a village located forty-five minutes from the city of Totonicapán. The oldest of four children, she lives with her mother and three siblings. The small, single-room adobe home is on loan to the family from her grandparents who live in an adjoining compound. The room is used for cooking and sleeping. Since joining the rug-hooking project, it's also where Rosmery creates her rugs.

When Rosmery was five years old, her mother announced that Rosmery would clean houses for neighbors. She would earn less than fifty cents a day, but every penny was needed to support their family. Then one day, when she was sixteen years old, she learned of an opportunity to travel by bus to Panajachel and participate in a new project. Her mom was not supportive. She thought Rosmery's time was better spent cleaning. But her beloved grandmother who lived in the same compound thought it was a good idea. She encouraged her participation and often gave Rosmery a few coins for transportation to class.

Rosmery remembers getting up at 4 a.m. feeling hopeful and excited as she traveled four hours by bus alone to attend her first rug-hooking class. "I didn't have confidence in my ability to do the work, but the other women, who were all older than me, said encouraging things to me. They made me feel I could do it."

Rosmery quickly discovered that she had a natural aptitude for rug hooking. She had never worked with colored pencils before, but she enjoyed learning to draw and plan her rug colors. For a young girl of sixteen, who attended school to the sixth grade, her trip to Pana was a determined first step on a journey that would see her graduate as the youngest of seven rug-hooking teachers.

Reflecting back on the teacher training course, she said, "When I learned that I would be a teacher, I felt afraid. I didn't have confidence, but my compañeras helped me. I especially remember Yolanda's good words of encouragement, and that made me feel I could do the work." She added, "The amount of information was tremendous. But each stage I felt that I could do it because of the way the information was given. Even though each procedure [step] has been difficult, we all learned it. To graduate with my mother in the audience was one of the proudest moments of my life."

Speaking about other transformations, she said, "Many girls in my village get married when they are thirteen or fourteen years old, but I want something different for myself. My life has changed. I discovered a talent I never knew I had. I feel positive about my life and I am more self-confident.

Rosmery Elizabeth Pacheco

With my rug money, we are saving to buy a small piece of land to build a better home." Smiling at me, knowing that I was aware of her former rocky relationship with her mother, she added, "I am now teaching my mother to hook rugs."

Speaking about her artistry, Rosmery grows animated and says, "My rugs express my feelings and every rug is part of my story. When I am away from my work it stays in my mind. I think about my design, if I can improve it, and I anticipate how I will change the design when I come back to it."

In spite of recent disappointments, such as having to drop out of an English language class to care for her bedridden grandfather who suffered a stroke, Rosmery is optimistic. In 2015, she was denied a visa during her interview at the U.S. embassy in Guatemala City and was therefore unable to represent her compañeras at the International Folk Art Market in Santa Fe, New Mexico. When I had a chance to ask Rosmery more details about her two visa application experiences, she said, "The first time when I traveled to the city, I was nervous and I felt scared—but for my second interview, my second trip to La Capital, I noticed the big buildings, so different from anything in my village, and I could see the beauty and some of the neighborhoods where people live and kids play outside. It is so different from where I live. Yes, the woman who interviewed me was rude; she didn't even look at my IFAM letter, and I think she was supposed to do that, wasn't she? When she told me to get out, she even called a policeman over to make sure I left." When I ask her about these setbacks, Rosmery said, "My disappoinments have made me stronger. I will travel one day and rug hooking will help me achieve my goals."

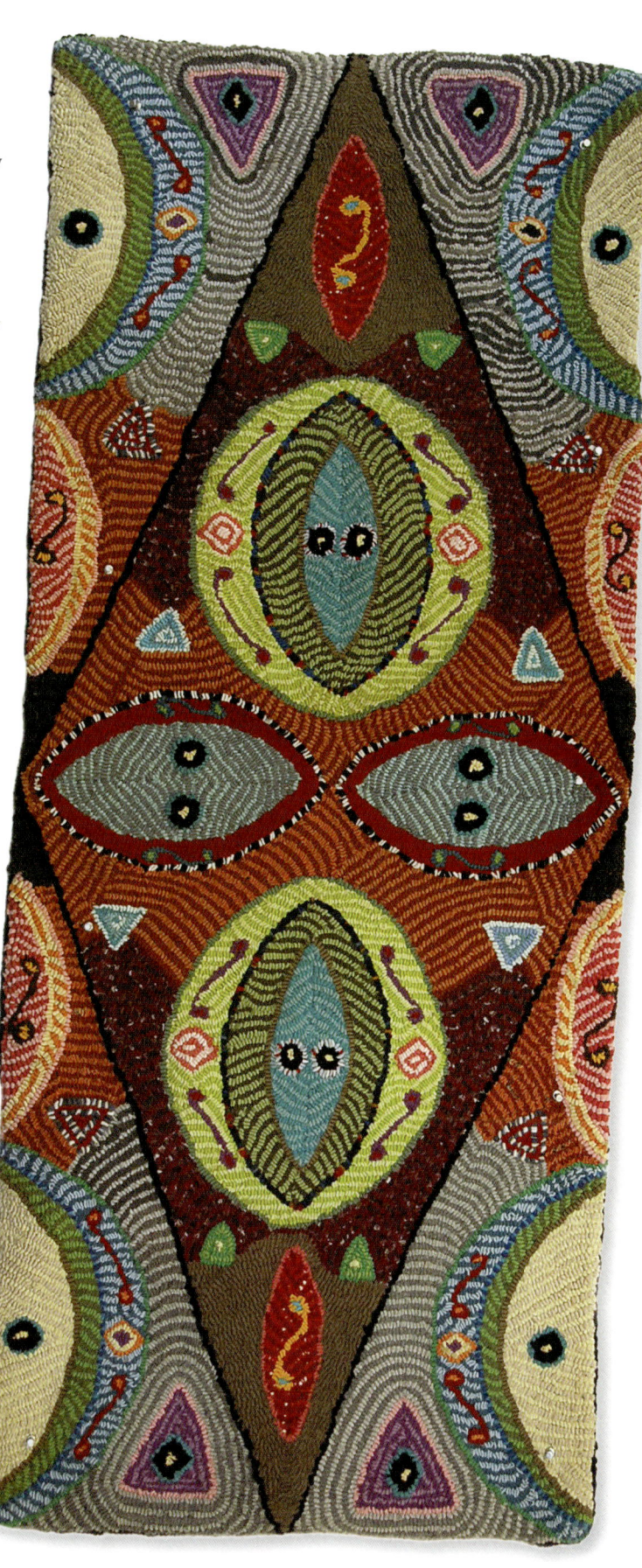

Rosmery Elizabeth Pacheco

The Teachers Teach
» OB Sala, Panajachel, Guatemala, October 30, 2012

The day after graduation, the teachers arrived with their students. Taking their seats at the table, the students were anxious and quiet. Few of the new recruits had ever participated in a class as adult women. The teachers stood to introduce themselves, their voices resonating kindness and confidence. Then the students shyly introduced themselves. A few of them, I noted, spoke into hands steepled at their mouths. Glendy stood before them and offered a warm welcome and words of encouragement. She told them, "I once sat where you are sitting. Do not worry, just try your best. We are here to help you and we will all move forward together." Then Carmen led a quick *dinámica*, a fun Simon Says-like game intended to break the ice. Reyna and I observed with pleasure as tensions were eased and everyone joined the game in laughter.

A thorough overview followed. Sindy introduced the design principles, explaining the meaning behind the icons for those who could not read. Yolanda and María Sacalxot explained how to draw a design on paper, María adding, "You will get to use color pencils in this class, too!" Zoila gave a demonstration on how to use the mirrors to envision more design possibilities, and Rosmery showed how to use templates adding, "This is something artists everywhere know how to do." María explained the characteristics of the correct paca cloth to choose and how to cut the cloth into strips. As a group, the teachers showed several rug examples and explained the ranking system of quality #1, #2, and #3, taking particular care to explain the payment according to the quality. Glendy said, "We don't expect you to memorize everything you saw here today. We are showing you our creative process so you can see some of the tools we have learned over many months. Just remember, when you go home, you must practice, practice, practice."

I worried that the new students were getting overwhelmed, but Reyna, catching on to my concern, pinned me in place with a look in her eyes that cautioned, "Let them handle this."

Cell phones kept ringing, interrupting the class, and Glendy asked them to please turn their phones off. Not twenty minutes went by when another phone rang and, to the intense displeasure of the new students, Glendy confiscated their phones. Reyna turned to me and smiled.

Finally, the students got busy drawing, often turning to Zoila for another demonstration of the mirror trick before picking up the mirrors to try for themselves. One of the new students, a very young mother, had brought her newborn daughter to class. It was her first child, and as the baby grew fussy, the young mother's agitation increased. She placed the baby on a pile of paca clothing, hoping the baby would sink into the soft pile and settle down to sleep, but the baby only squealed louder. Glendy picked up the infant and nonchalantly bundled it in her tzute, then tied the baby to her back as she continued her lecture uninterrupted. The baby quieted. Watching Glendy, I thought, "Rug hooking is not the only thing we are teaching today."

Amazing color work frames a classic bird motif. OPPOSITE ABOVE: Rug in process. OPPOSITE BELOW: A gathering of Multicolores artists.

78   An Extraordinary Opportunity

As the afternoon came to a close, the teachers assigned homework. Carmen reminded the students, "It is your responsibility to gather everything you need to complete your assignment before you leave this classroom." Predictably, Glendy was first to grab the broom as others joined in and tidied the classroom. Leaving the sala, the teachers accompanied their students to a nearby hotel where they would spend the evening together as a group. I knew tonight would be the first time most of the new students had been away from home, likely their first time staying at a hotel, and perhaps their first experience eating at a restaurant. They would wander up Santander and they would take in the sights before going back to their rooms. They would stop to buy an ice cream, for as I watched them depart from the sala, I spied Reyna slipping one of the teachers money for this rare treat. I knew the women would laugh and gossip into the night, like always. I felt confident they would do their homework because none of them would dare disappoint her teacher.

The next day, the new students would begin their first rugs. They would return home with ideas dancing in their heads and with minds numb from absorbing so much information. Just like Carmen—and all the teachers—the motivated new students would master the craft. They would reach within and find the will to latch on to this extraordinary opportunity and alter the trajectory of their lives. By 2016, fifty-eight women had done just that.

» Artists of the Patanatic Rug-Hooking Group

TOP ROW, LEFT TO RIGHT: Glendy, Sheny, Irma, Juana, Nicolasa, Lucia. BOTTOM ROW, LEFT TO RIGHT: Roxana, Virginia, Eva, Bartola, Silvia.

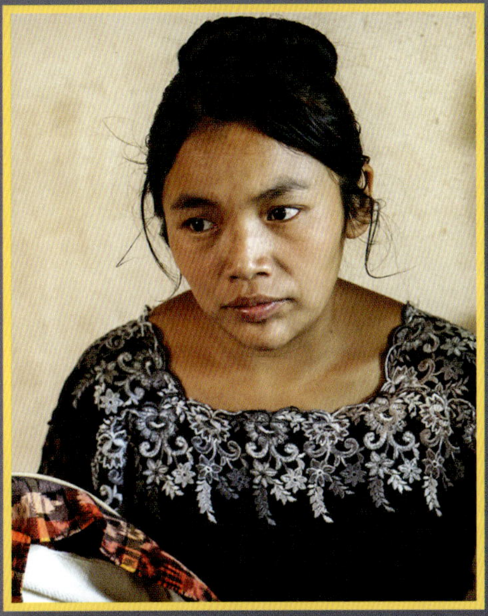
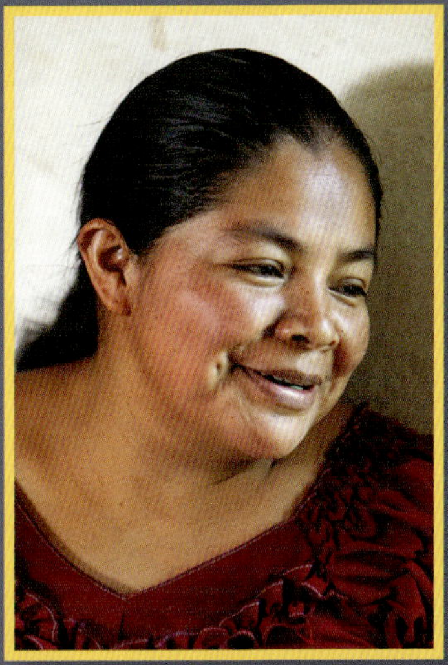
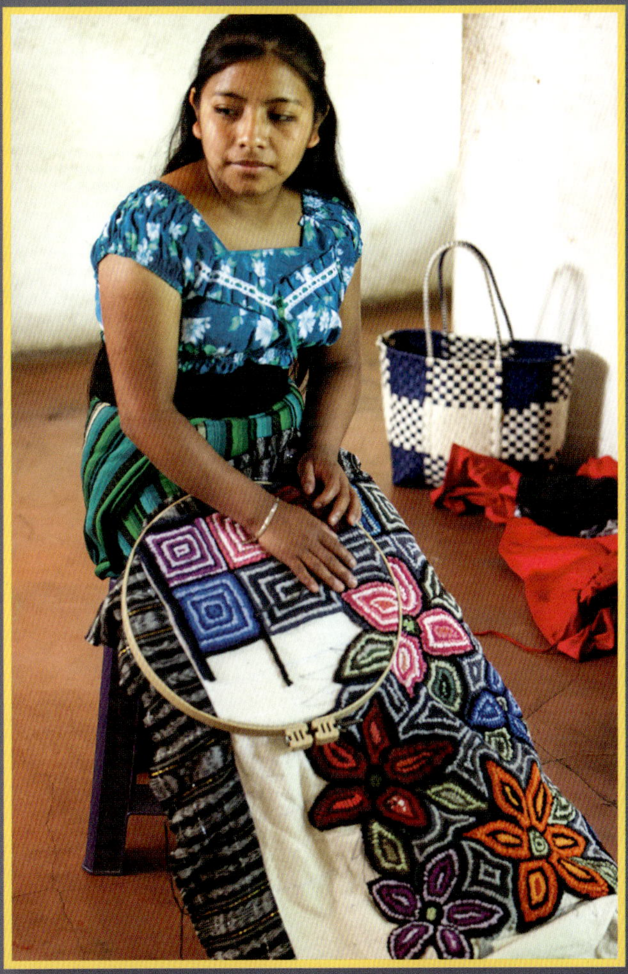
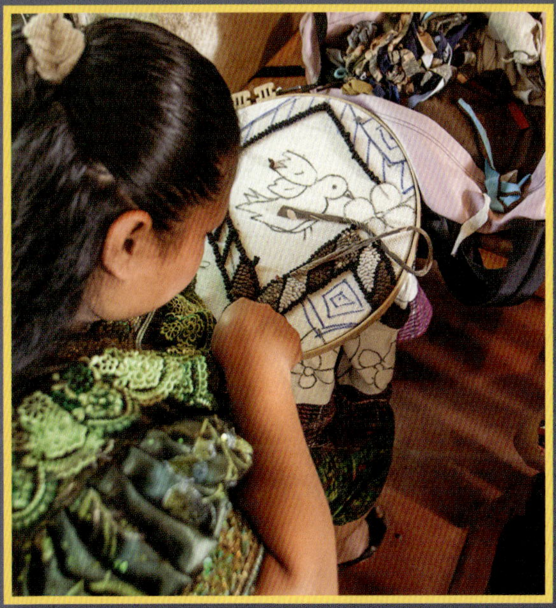
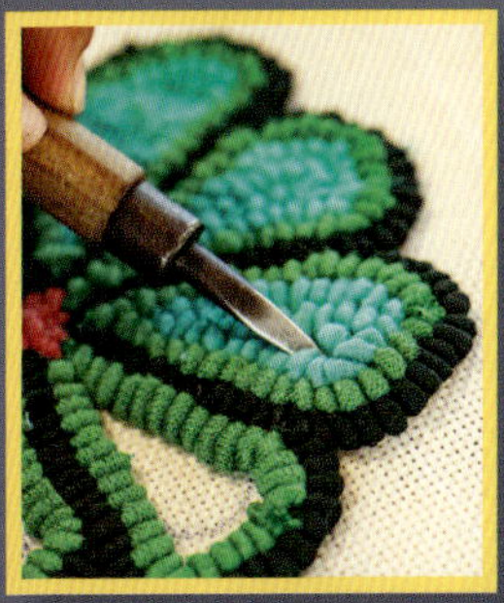

» Artists of the Totonicapán Rug-Hooking Group

TOP ROW, LEFT TO RIGHT: Leandra, Rosmery, Dolores, Hilda, Juana. BOTTOM ROW, LEFT TO RIGHT: Gloria, Rosario, Nicolasa, Ramona.

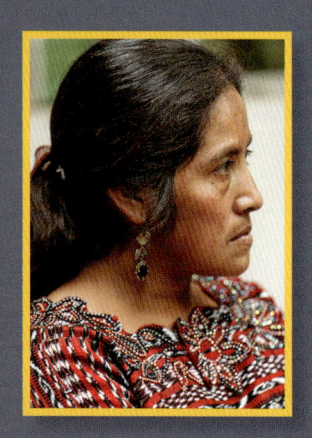

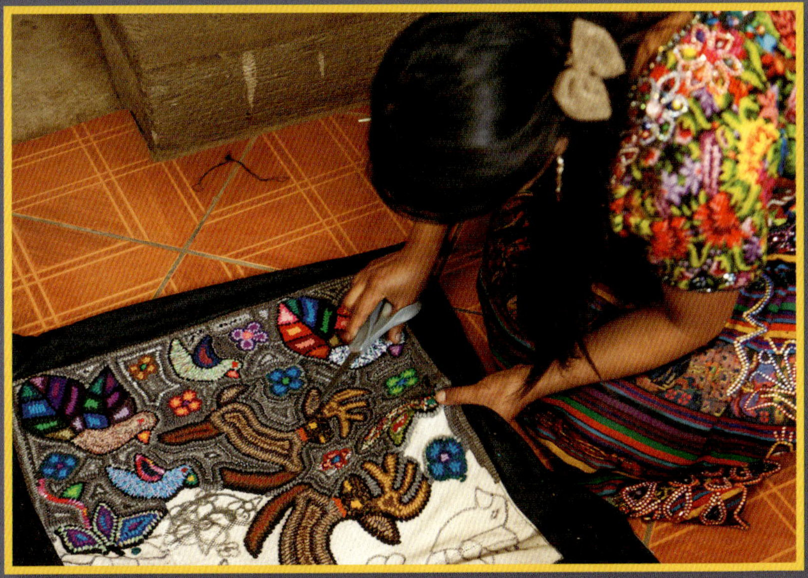
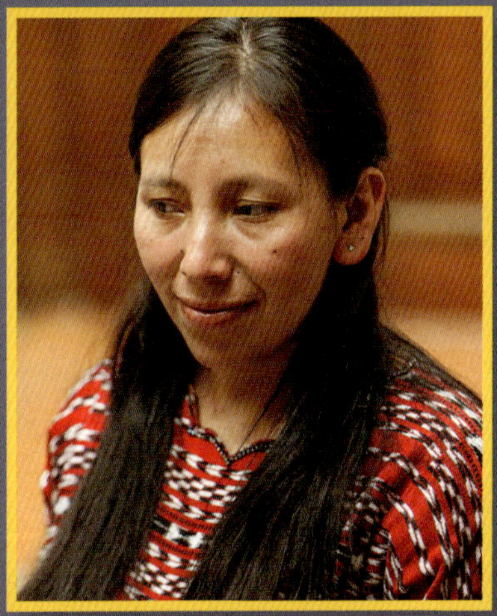
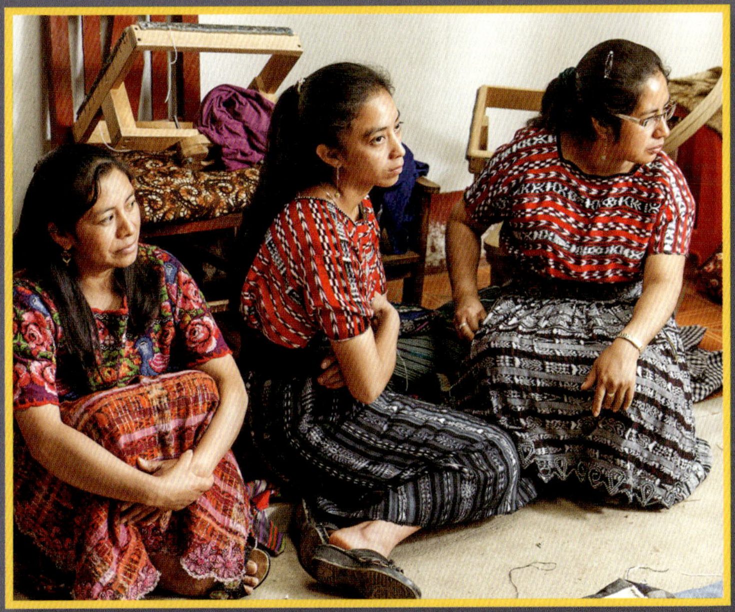
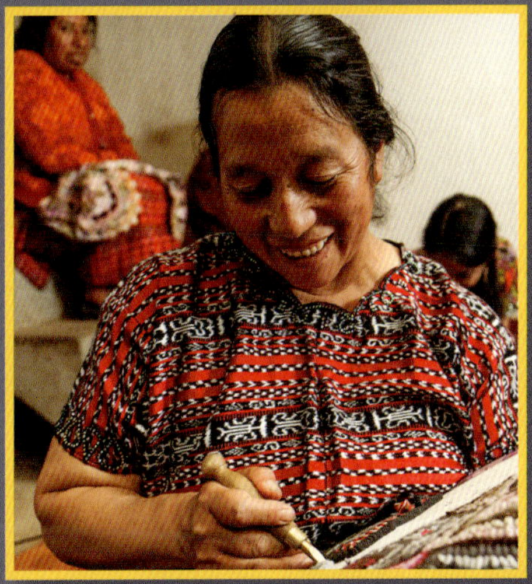
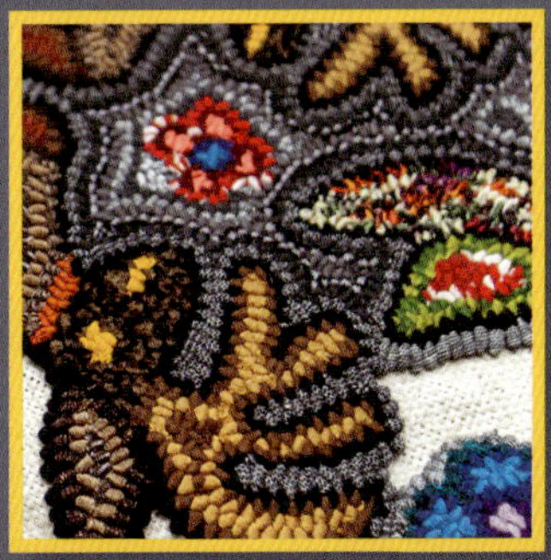

» Artists of the Quiejel Rug-Hooking Group

LEFT TO RIGHT: Yessika, Silvia, Lesly, Petronila, Ana Mariela, Tomasa. SEATED: Yolanda, Maricela.

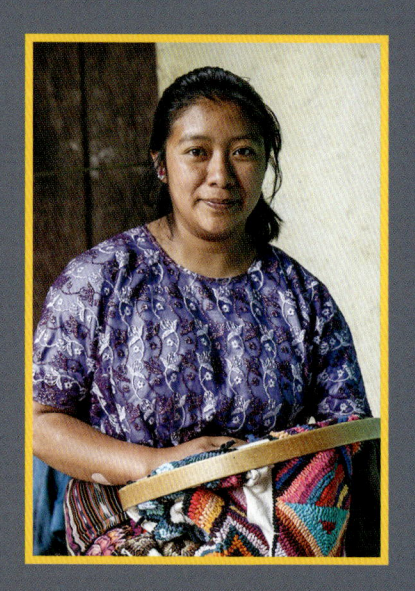

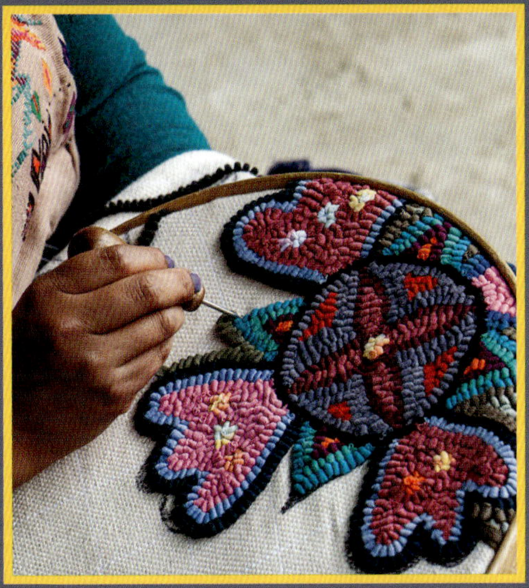
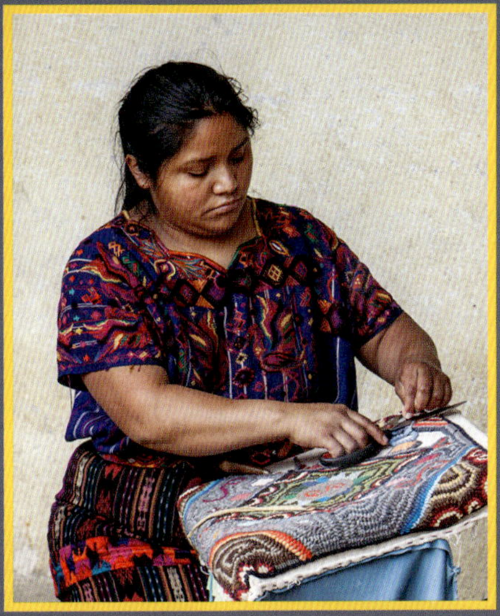
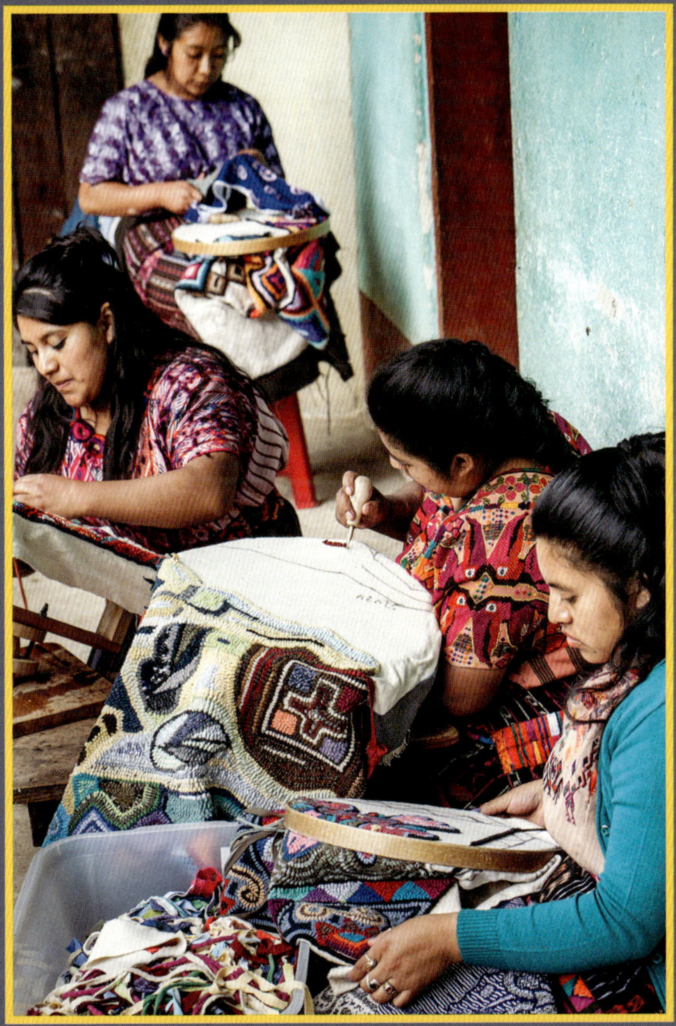
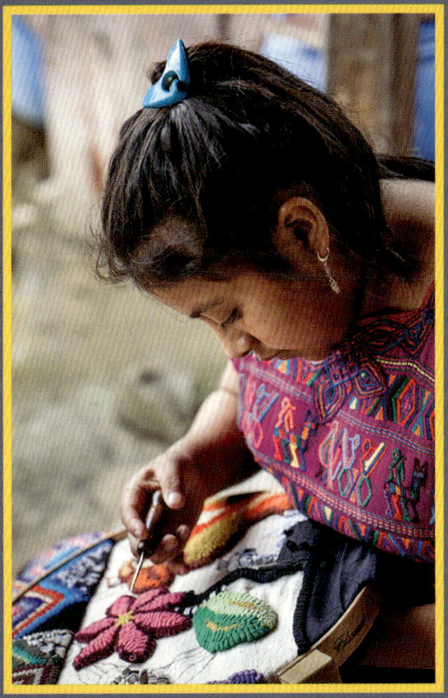

Part 11:
The Color of Success

The First Intercambio Session (Guatemala's Largest Rug Hook-in)
» Reyna's Apartment and Hotel Kaqchiquel,
  Panajachel, Guatemala, August 2013

For the previous few months, Yolanda had performed her job as roving rug-hooking ambassador. She traveled to the rug-hooking communities to check on the progress made by the new teachers and their students. Reporting back to Reyna and Cheryl, they learned that some of the groups had issues of leadership that needed to be straightened out. Reyna and Cheryl decided that the best way to accomplish this was for all the students and their teachers to come together as a group. Working from Reyna's apartment, because they did not yet have an official "office," the two met to plan our first *intercambio* (exchange) session. In addition to addressing group issues, the session would be a chance for Reyna to determine the artistic progress made by those new to rug hooking. Added to the mix was the need to gauge rug production levels because we had decided to explore the possibility of applying to the International Folk Art Market in Santa Fe. The Market's lengthy application was due in six weeks.

Forty-eight rug hookers came together for the weekend-long session at Hotel Kaqchiquel. It was the biggest hook-in ever hosted in Guatemala! Reyna planned the program and included a discussion on color and quality control. In addition, she wanted a speaker, an experienced rug hooker, to present to the gathering. She wanted someone who would motivate the attendees and encourage them to take advantage of the opportunities of the rug-hooking program. She chose Carmen because, of all the participants in the program thus far, Carmen had overcome the most obstacles.

Standing before the audience, Reyna introduced Carmen. Pausing only a moment to take in the sea of faces before her, Carmen addressed the group. She spoke in a clear voice that was audible from the back of the long banquet room where I sat. She said she was pleased to speak to them, her compañeras, and she expressed gratitude for Reyna and Cheryl's dedication to the project, and for Jody's and my help over the years. She thanked God for the opportunity to participate in the rug-hooking program. She did not dwell on her hardships, her poverty, or lack of education, or that her husband abandoned her when their children were small many years ago. Instead, she talked about the confusing process to learn this technique and how, at first, she didn't have any ideas for designs much less know how to draw them. Pointing to herself, she said, "But I stuck with it and I discovered things about myself I didn't know were there." She continued on, encouraging everyone in the room to help one another and to stick with it, saying, "If I can learn this? You can, too." Before closing, she offered some practical advice, "Work specific hours every day because a routine will help you finish your rug. When you complete your rug, you can get paid right away—and that is a very good feeling." As she left the stage, she singled out Zoila and recommended that the students speak to her because "she is very good with colors."

And then it was time for the throw-down! Everyone untied their tzutes and unfurled their rugs onto the floor. Soon there was no room to walk, except on rugs, and so we spilled out of the banquet hall and onto the patio and then into the hotel lobby as still more rugs appeared. Looking at the astounding array of rugs, my gaze connected with Cheryl. I knew what she was thinking: "Yes, we could be prepared for the quantity of rugs necessary for the Folk Art Market."

Petronila demonstrates her rug-hooking skills and her instinctive sense of color.

Participants in Guatemala's largest rug hook-in. OPPOSITE: Zoila unfurls her masterpiece—a 5-by-7-foot rug, the central design inspired by Todos Santos kites.

I felt especially eager to see a large 5-by-7-foot rug I'd commissioned from Zoila six months earlier. Zoila's designs had become increasingly complex, full of many ideas within a single rug. "If we challenged her with a larger format, what might she create?" I wondered. "Masterpiece" was the evident answer, because when she unfurled her rug at my feet, my heart nearly stopped beating. Her rug referenced *barriletes* (colorfully detailed kites constructed of tissue paper for *Todos Santos*, All Saints Festival) and the cardinal points were surrounded by a constellation of dizzying pattern. Her rug was an extraordinary accomplishment. As the women gathered around to admire her rug, it was apparent to all that Zoila had broken new ground.

More than a year later, Reyna would invite six of the best rug designers to our new office in Panajachel for a workshop on large-format rug designs. Ramona Tumax would lead the workshop.

When asked to reflect on her first large-format rug design, Zoila rolls her eyes. *When you told me the size you wanted I couldn't believe I heard you right. I thought there was no way I could ever finish a rug that big. I would have gray hair (like you!) before I was done. But then you gave me the big piece of ground cloth, and then I started getting ideas, and somehow I worked on it until it was done. When it was done, I thought 'never again.' But now I think differently about the big rugs; they are impressive, I admit, and there is a sense of accomplishment with all I put into them.*

Applying to the International Folk Art Market
» Panajachel, Guatemala; Wisconsin, USA;
   Belfast, Northern Ireland, September 2013

Following the intercambio session, we kicked into gear and began to parse out the tasks necessary to complete the International Folk Art Market application. We had been dreaming of applying for several years, yet we didn't feel confident that we were fully prepared. And so we approached the application as if it were an exercise that would be "good practice." Next year, we reasoned, we would be better prepared with more experience, and that's when we would have a better chance of being accepted. Still, the question of sufficient inventory had clearly been answered. The choice of Artist Representative—the individual whose name would appear on the application as the group's representative—was more complicated. Among the rug hookers, Yolanda alone had acquired a passport when she traveled to the Anderson Center exhibition two years earlier. Nearly as significant, she had a history of being granted a visa for that same trip. In spite of a language barrier, she was also outgoing and able to easily connect with people. This characteristic, we knew, meant she would be good at sales at the Market. We concluded that if by some miracle we got accepted, Yolanda's chances of being granted a second visa were good. We discussed giving the travel opportunity to another woman, but getting a passport takes time. Factor in the necessary travel time and expense to Guatemala City, along with the cost of the visa, and the price per applicant is about $460. With limited funds and the application deadline looming, Yolanda was the obvious candidate.

Cheryl worked on the application forms from her home in Northern Ireland. In Wisconsin, I worked on organizing the photos of rugs required to accompany the application. In Guatemala, Reyna worked on rallying the women. As we completed the application, emails to one another flew back and forth. At last I dispatched the thick document via overnight express mail, for we had worked right up to the deadline. At the Folk Art Market's office in Santa Fe, our application would be processed along with nearly 400 other hopeful artists from 77 countries. Only 170 applicants representing 62 countries would receive an affirmative reply.

Holding my flashlight on January first, I descended the rickety basement steps at Cultural Cloth's shop in Maiden Rock, Wisconsin. I was feeling frustrated coupled with a sense of dread because the pipes had frozen, and I feared what I would find in the dark below. My cell phone rang. Fumbling with the lantern as I answered the call, I heard Jody's excited shouts, "We got in! We got in! I just talked to Reyna and she received the acceptance letter from the Folk Art Market!" Her news instantly filled me with joy, immediately followed by a more sober thought, "Could we do it?" Ricocheting back to joy—for look what we had achieved already—my heart began to fill with a sense of lightness and infinite appreciation for all we had accomplished together as the faces of Jody and Reyna and Cheryl and Yolanda and Carmen and Glendy and Rosmery and Ramona T. and on and on paraded through my mind. I felt hopeful and even triumphant.

The International Folk Art Market
» Panajachel, Guatemala; Santa Fe, New Mexico, USA, January–July 2014

The International Folk Art Market (IFAM) is nearly impossible to explain—it should be experienced. It takes place outdoors under massive tents on Museum Hill located in a quiet residential area, about ten minutes from the downtown plaza in Santa Fe, New Mexico. It occurs over two and a half days and attracts twenty thousand people who come with one purpose in mind: to buy art. Over fifteen hundred volunteers help run the event along with a staff of fewer than twenty full-time employees. The day before the Market opens, the city of Santa Fe turns out to welcome the artists. The Market throws a big dance party. Throngs of visitors and locals enjoy live music and a parade that rivals the opening ceremony at the Olympics for its global scope. All the Market artists, dressed in their traditional clothing, form a long line as the official announcer introduces them before cheering crowds. Tall Masai men march alongside petite women from Malaysia, artists from the Congo queue behind those from Colombia. It's a stirring sight. Santa Fe residents feel so proud of so many cultures and countries coming together in their city, they like to say, "This peace-filled event could only happen in Santa Fe."

Back in Guatemala, in preparation for the Market, Reyna was busy making community visits to check on rug production and quality. She encouraged the women to work hard to meet this extraordinary opportunity. Multicolores pledged to purchase all their rugs outright, using a loan backed by Jody and me. The women would also receive a bonus on each of their rugs sold in Santa Fe.

We assumed that we had at least six months to fulfill our inventory target because the Market didn't occur until July. But upon learning more about the Market's rules, we now understood that the bulk of our inventory must arrive in Santa Fe before the end of April, about four months away. This new information gave Reyna an even greater sense of urgency. Then slowly, one by one, the women began to arrive in Panajachel, knocking at her apartment door, carrying their rugs wrapped in tzutes tied to their backs or balanced on their heads. Before the artists returned home, Reyna would evaluate, document, pay for, photograph, and affix a price tag to each and every rug.

Meanwhile, in Northern Ireland and in Wisconsin, Cheryl, Jody, and I anxiously awaited Reyna's emails, eager to learn how the rug deliveries were proceeding. Day by day, we witnessed proof of her progress in time-lapse photos. We watched with an expanding sense of ease as her small apartment filled to overflowing with stacks upon stacks of rugs. Reyna soon announced that she had met the halfway mark in our required inventory level and was ready to ship. While this first batch of rugs was making its way to the United States, the rug hookers continued working on the second batch of rugs to be shipped in mid-May. Reyna quipped that rugs completed after the final ship date "could even be stuffed into checked luggage," and indeed, some rugs were.

Dozens of rugs pile up in Reyna's apartment in preparation for shipping to Santa Fe.

Reyna brought 252 rugs to the market and most of them, or so it seemed, were piled high on top of the booth's two tables—piled to the point of near collapse. But with Reyna unpacking still more rugs, we grabbed a couple of abandoned wooden pallets and stashed them under our tables. Knowing that afternoon rainstorms are a staple of New Mexican summers, we hoped to have just enough ground clearance to keep the rugs dry. Then suddenly the moment arrived. The Market opened, and we watched as the multitudes kept coming and coming and coming some more. Soon our small 10-by-10-foot booth was full of customers and Yolanda greeted them with a sincere smile and her few words of English, "Welcome! Hello, my name is Yolanda. I am from Quiejel, Guatemala."

At home in Guatemala, Yolanda would often face discrimination for the color of her skin. But while in Santa Fe, she was feted by adoring crowds for the fact that she was a Folk Art Market artist. Posters of her face, advertising the Market, plastered the city. She saw the posters all over the place. The tables had turned. It was a bit overwhelming. And also brilliantly validating.

Yolanda representing the rug-hooking project at its debut at the International Folk Art Market.

At the close of the market only two rugs remained. The women of Multicolores had sold 250 rugs.

In reflecting upon her experience at the International Folk Art Market, Yolanda said:

I became the famous one through all the publicity we got as rug hookers; that was such a surprise and so amazing, it made me feel very good. I felt so proud to be able to work the booth and help sell the rugs. When the market was over, there were only two rugs left. I was also surprised to see such high-quality crafts at the market; it's something I'll never forget. I know we must always work our hardest to maintain the quality. Oh! And the volunteers. Be sure to say how surprised I was by the volunteers—we don't have that in Guatemala. I keep imagining ways we could do that [create volunteers] in my country.

The Color of Success

Visiting the Communities and Choosing the
2015 International Folk Art Market Artist Representative
» Multicolores Office, Panajachel; Guatemala Highlands, January 2015

By now, all of the rug hookers had received their bonuses from sales at the International Folk Art Market, and Jody and I had been repaid our earlier loan. We had applied—and were accepted—for a second year at the IFAM. Fueled in part by sales at the Market, Multicolores was positioned to grow. The organization was able to move out of Reyna's apartment and rent a small house as an office. We committed to inviting more women into the program and training them as rug hookers, holding classes in the communities and follow-up sessions in the new office.

Next, Reyna and Cheryl established a paid intern program to help relieve Reyna of some of her time-consuming tasks. Rosmery became an intern. Her home was located nearly four hours from Pana and therefore, during her bimonthly intern stints, she stayed at the office, sleeping in the spare bedroom. We knew Rosmery had a difficult home life and working under Reyna's mentorship, we reasoned she might begin to envision new possibilities. We also thought she would grow more confidence and that would be useful when she traveled to the U.S. the following summer, because she had been honored as the IFAM Artist Representative for 2015.

Jody and I were back in Guatemala for a fourth rug-hooking tour. Tours had become an important fundraiser for Multicolores. Reyna suggested that in addition to the tour, we also build in time to travel into the communities. Sixty-two women were now hooking rugs and Jody and I had only met half of them. We could meet the new rug hookers and if time allowed, we would conduct critiques, too. In addition to critiquing their rugs, we could observe the dynamics of the group and follow up later, if necessary, to address concerns. Equally important, community visits gave us a better understanding of the challenges the women faced in their daily lives.

Our first visit was Totonicapán where Rosmery was the teacher. En route, Reyna fielded several of her phone calls wondering, "Where are you?" And ten minutes later, she phoned again, asking, "How close are you now?" Upon arriving, the urgency of her repeated phone calls was clear: they had timed our arrival to welcome us with a hot lunch that included meat. As guests of honor, we were directed to sit at the table on the few available chairs and we would be served first.

After our meal, as some cleared dishes, the others began arranging rugs for the throw-down. The women who knew me understood that this was the moment I'd been impatiently awaiting. Jody and I immediately noted improved craftsmanship and that their designs kept evolving. It was exciting to see! Next came the critiques. Noting the clock, Cheryl suggested we combine the critiques with her planned interviews of the rug hookers. In her ongoing efforts to collect empirical data for the project, Cheryl queried the women for basic demographics, additionally asking what each one did prior to rug hooking and how she had benefited from her rug money.

The two of us positioned ourselves in a corner for privacy and spoke to each woman one by one. Cheryl, I knew, would unobtrusively ask her questions amidst my critique comments. But their rugs were so impressive that I had little to suggest except to congratulate them on mastering rug hooking, to ask about their design inspiration, and to express my genuine admiration for their artistry. One woman

Rosmery was chosen as the Artist Representative at the 2015 International Folk Art Market.

after another told us a similar story: "I am thirty-eight years old, and I never thought of myself as an artist, but I do now. It is a good feeling to know I have this talent."

The last person to critique was fifty-three-year-old Marta Pérez. She had participated in the early classes, and it was generally understood that what Marta lacked in rug-hooking skills she made up for in determination. Unable to grasp design concepts or use of color, her friends would draw her designs and choose her colors and that is how her rugs got made. After discussing her rug, Cheryl asked, "Marta, please remind me how many children you have. I've forgotten."

Marta's face crumbled as tears spilled from her eyes. "I have two sons, and I don't know where my daughter is. She paid a coyote three years ago but no one ever heard from her after she left. Her friends in the U.S. never heard from her, and I haven't heard from her either. I don't know if she is alive or dead."

Almost everyone we know and work with has an immediate family member living in the United States. They leave their homeland because they run out of options to earn a living, and they feel desperate to support their families. The route into the U.S. is extremely dangerous, infested with narcotics traffickers and gang members. I'd read of tragic stories along this route, including rape and murder. But Marta was the first acquaintance I knew who had lost a loved one in this lawless territory.

Before leaving and heading to our next destination, Reyna had a surprise announcement. Today we would award cash prizes of Q150 and above (about $20.50 or the equivalent of nearly three days' wages for an uneducated, unskilled rural Guatemalan woman). We awarded prizes to the two women who had produced the most rugs during the previous year and in each of the now four rug-hooking communities to the women whose quality ranking had improved the most.

Reyna's approach to the awards seemed equitable, I noted, because the categories included a possible reward for those who had been in the program for several years and also one for those who were fairly new. Glendy and Carmen received awards for their impressive rug production. Improved artists included Tomasa, María Estela, Rosa, Juana, and Irma. Reyna asked me to present the prizes as she called each woman forward to stand before their group. When it was Rosa's turn, Reyna had presented her complimentary remarks, and I was just about to place the money in her hand when Rosa's cell phone rang. She darted out of the room. Surprised by her quick disappearance, I exchanged looks with Reyna that said, "Really? She has someone better to speak to

The Multicolores office down a quiet pedestrian street, just off busy Santander Street in Panajachel. BELOW: An extraordinary rug by Micaela features a multi-dimensional border and a design clearly drawn from brocade weaving.

The Color of Success 93

than me who is about to give her nearly half a week's worth of wages? What could be more important?"

Rosa's caller, I later learned, was her fifteen-year-old son, Juan. Two weeks ago, the family paid a coyote to take him to the U.S. Well aware of the dangers he would encounter and knowing what had happened to her friend Marta's daughter, ever since his departure, she had worried herself nearly sick. But today's phone call was good news: Juan was calling to let her know he had arrived safely. He was phoning from his uncle's home in Houston.

On the drive back to the office, we discussed the timeline for Rosmery's visa. The visa applicant is required to appear in person for an interview at the U.S. embassy in Guatemala City. She must present her passport along with supporting letters of invitation from U.S. organizations or citizens to substantiate the reason for the visit. In 2015, the International Folk Art Market accepted four applicants from Guatemala. Out of a population of sixteen million people, four Guatemalan citizens received official letters of invitation from the IFAM. Rosmery was one of them. She had her papers in order, she had a passport, and now she could apply for a visa. Reyna made the appointment.

Accompanied by Reyna, they arrived at the U.S. embassy for Rosmery's visa interview. While Reyna waited in the reception area, Rosmery entered the interview room where only the applicant is allowed. Barely two minutes passed when Rosmery, looking flushed and agitated, rejoined Reyna—her application had been denied. With aspiring applicants looking on, Reyna quickly gathered their belongings and made a hasty departure. Outside the embassy Reyna asked, "What happened?"

Shaken, Rosmery replied, "She asked me if I was married and if I had children. I said no. And that was all. She didn't look at my letters of invitation and she told me to get out. I was so surprised at what was happening, I think I was in shock; I just sat there another minute until she yelled at me again to move."

Learning this news in Northern Ireland, Cheryl immediately contacted the IFAM office for suggestions on how to help Rosmery. In Wisconsin, Jody reached out to our U.S. senator, Tammy Baldwin, asking her to intervene, and she did. Finally, Rosmery was granted a nearly unprecedented second interview. Traveling once again to the city, she arrived at the embassy feeling a mixture of hope, determination, and intimidation. But she was assigned the same embassy official who simply looked up and said, "Oh, it's you again. Get out," and she stamped her application "Denied." She never looked at Rosmery's papers.

Rosmery's second visa denial meant that we needed to quickly vet another candidate as Artist Representative. Knowing it took several weeks, or longer, to receive a passport and apply for a visa, the calendar was running out. We decided to spread our risk and pay for two rug hookers to get passports, reasoning that surely one of them would get a visa. Conferring with one another through a flurry of emails, we agreed that either Carmen or Glendy would do a great job as Artist Representative. With passports in hand, the two compañeras, by now old friends, traveled together to the city for their embassy interviews. Glendy was denied immediately; the reason was unclear. Carmen was next. Ten minutes later she exited the interview room wearing a wide smile and holding her visa.

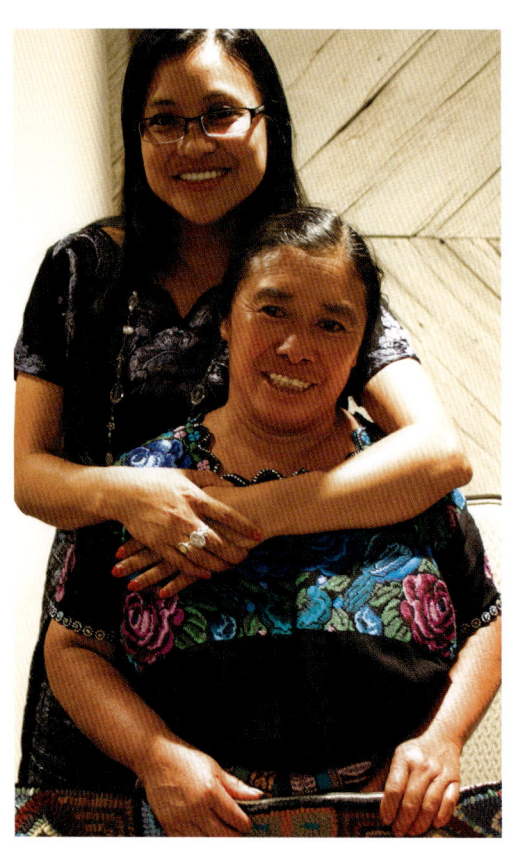

Reyna with Carmen who represented Multicolores at the International Folk Art Market in 2015. OPPOSITE: After learning to hook rugs from Yolanda and Glendy, Micaela quickly excelled in her rug design and craftsmanship.

Carmen Represents Her Compañeras at the International Folk Art Market
» Santa Fe, New Mexico, USA, April–July 2015

Reyna was less concerned about production levels this year because by now the women understood the benefits of producing for the Market. They would get paid up front and receive bonuses if their rugs sold. They felt invested in their success and they were making steady progress on their rugs. They also understood that a portion of the profits would help fund Multicolores. Multicolores was beginning to mean something to the artists who made the connection between the work Reyna and Cheryl performed and the improvements to their lives.

As rug deliveries increased and the rugs accumulated at the office, including half a dozen large rugs by new artists, we discussed the possibility of bringing all the women together for a second intercambio session. The quality of their craftsmanship had improved; indeed, Reyna rarely saw rugs ranked quality #3. We understood the value of inviting all of the women from five communities to come together as a single organization united in purpose. There was a lot to be gained from viewing the astounding array of rugs and they would be inspired by their collective accomplishment. We knew we'd have to pay the women's travel expenses and there was no money in the budget for this sudden expenditure. That thought was immediately followed by the knowledge that our generous North American tour alums could relate to this endeavor. Our tour alumni—many of whom are serious rug hookers— would appreciate the value of viewing an inspiring body of work. They enjoy this opportunity at annual hook-in events throughout the U.S. and Canada. Cheryl sent out a plea and shortly thereafter, the alumni, and several U.S.-based rug-hooking groups responded. The intercambio was funded.

The intercambio also provided a collegial and supportive environment to energize the artists. It was an opportunity for those who might work at a lesser quality to see, touch, and experience high quality. For the ones who thought it was impossible to improve—they could be inspired by a conversation with someone who had improved her quality. To address the quality issue, Reyna chose Micaela to speak to the group. Micaela, who learned rug hooking from Yolanda and Glendy, had been hooking rugs for less than two years, but her quality of craftsmanship and design was excellent. Micaela was a motivated woman, and Reyna wanted to recognize her talent as a way to build her confidence and inspire others to achieve even more.

Finally, the time to depart for the Folk Art Market arrived. Arriving in Santa Fe, Reyna accompanied Carmen to the Market Readiness sessions. The readiness sessions are held just before the Market opens and are designed to help first-time participants succeed at the Market. Carmen quickly made acquaintances with artists from Spanish-speaking countries. That evening, Carmen, as a guest of honor, attended a Market kickoff party hosted by JoAnn Balzer, a member of IFAM's board of directors, and her husband Bob. Carmen's entourage, Reyna, Cheryl, Jody, and me, all tagged along, riding her coattails. Also in attendance, the mayor of Santa Fe Javier Gonzales, speaking in Spanish, welcomed Carmen to Santa Fe and told her, "My house is your house." Carmen beamed and took it in.

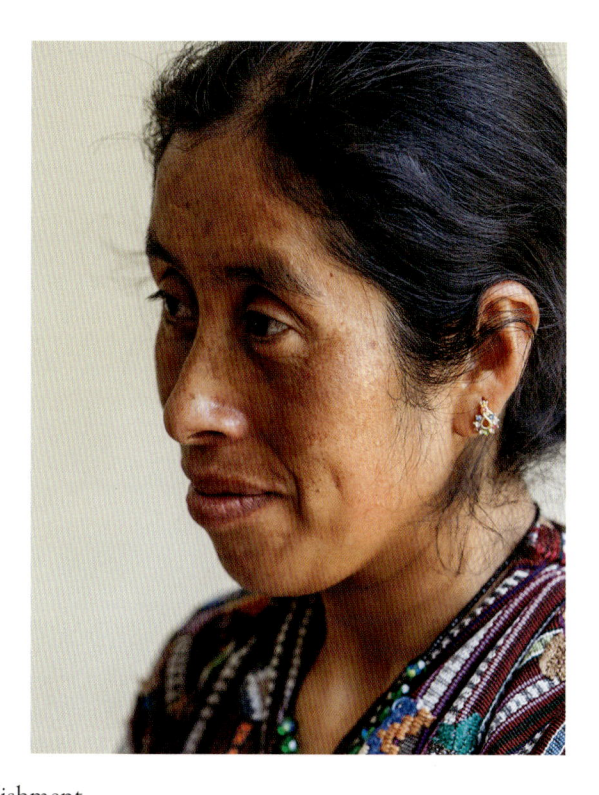

The day before the Market opened, Carmen participated alongside Dahyalal Kudecha, a weaver from Bhuj, Gujarat, India, as one of two artists presenting their work at a panel discussion hosted by the Textile Society of America. Carmen spoke about the impact of the rug-hooking program upon her life and explained the significance of the rug designs. Observing her presentation from my seat at the back of the room, it was clear Carmen held the audience in her hand. At the conclusion of the discussion, she worked the crowd, mingling with attendees and distributing her business card imprinted with our Market booth number. Turning to Cheryl and Jody, we all smiled in satisfaction, shaking our heads in wonder. There was no need for words.

When the Market opened and the throngs of attendees kept pouring through the gates, Carmen took in the site of the ceaseless crowds, repeatedly asking Reyna, "Are all these people really here to buy art?" The day before, an article written by Anne Constable appeared in the *Santa Fe New Mexican* newspaper and featured a story about the IFAM, including an interview with Carmen. Now those readers were stopping by our booth to have their photo taken next to Carmen, who beamed. She expressed surprise at how the buyers were genuinely interested in the rugs and answered question after question about how they were made: "Is this really recycled clothing?" "The transformation is incredible!" Over and over, Carmen explained the significance of the designs and the process. She was impressed by the rotation of Market volunteers who regularly stopped at each booth to offer encouraging words and water and free food! Sandwich in hand, she turned to Cheryl and explained, shaking her head, "You would never get free food in Guatemala!"

Carmen and I took a break from our busy stall to walk around the market together. We stopped at booths to admire the quality of this or marvel at that or exchange friendly quips with other Spanish-speaking participants. Finding some shade, we paused and I sat down on a ledge. I had a question I'd been meaning to ask. Hopping up to sit next to me, she said, "*Digame*" (tell me). I reminded her of a statement she made several years ago, a statement about her being a low person because that is how people see you if you don't write or haven't been to school. Continuing, I said, "Help me understand how people see you now, Carmen."

Smiling like a Cheshire cat she replied, "*Piensan que soy inteligente*." (They think I'm intelligent.)

Reyna and Cheryl with Carmen in Multiclores's booth at the International Folk Art Market in Santa Fe. OPPOSITE: Carmen, happy at home with Scooby Doo.

Carmen's Journey Home
» Minneapolis, Minnesota, USA; Maiden Rock, Wisconsin, USA; Chirijquiac, Guatemala, July 2015

After a nearly three-week visit to the United States, Carmen was ready to go home. At the IFAM she had represented her compañeras brilliantly. Packing up the booth after the Market was over, she gave Reyna tips to convey to the next Artist Representative, if we got accepted again. "They must smile, be friendly, and be enthusiastic so they can sell a lot of rugs!"

Carmen and Cheryl followed Jody and me home to Wisconsin where Carmen taught a rug-hooking workshop. She was impressed by "how nice all the students treated me—even when they got frustrated." At a fundraiser hosted by friends in Minneapolis, Carmen spoke of her life before rug hooking and her transformational experiences after she learned the technique. At Cultural Cloth's shop in Maiden Rock, Wisconsin, she demonstrated rug hooking to our customers. Meeting our customers, she felt happy because "they want to talk to me and even tell their children to say hi to me." She wanted to know if there were pacas in the U.S. So Cheryl, accompanied by a tour alum, scoured the Twin Cities' best used-clothing stores. Carmen made many purchases, although the paca was not intended for her rugs, it was for gifts. She was surprised to watch Jody's husband, Kurt, and my husband, Arne, help with cooking and dishwashing. Afterward, she made a note to talk to her younger son. "He will have to be more helpful. I am not going to serve him all the time anymore." She confided to Cheryl that she couldn't wait to get home to make tortillas, and she wondered why Americans liked to eat so many vegetables that were not cooked.

Arriving at Aurora International Airport in Guatemala City, Carmen was met by an entourage of family and her best friend and neighbor, María Sacalxot, one of the seven rug-hooking teachers. Together since 2009, the two longtime friends participated in every class Jody, Reyna, and I taught, including the teacher training sessions. More than anyone, María understood the victories her friend had achieved. She would not miss this opportunity to witness and celebrate Carmen's triumphant return. Leaving La Capital behind, as their journey to Chirijquiac stretched before them, Carmen answered their rapid-fire questions, joking and laughing and telling stories of her travels. She felt a sense of satisfaction and luxuriated in the quiet contentment of travelers everywhere who anticipate home with a sense of pleasure. She missed her dog, Scooby Doo, and she missed her house, and nearing her village she felt flooded with relief to be surrounded again by familiar fields of corn.

The Color of Success

» Artists of the Chirijquiac Rug-Hooking Group

LEFT TO RIGHT: Maria Estela, Maria Sacalxot, Paula, Tomasa, Pascuala, Maria Ignacia, Carmen. TOP ROW: Elizabeth, Carmen.

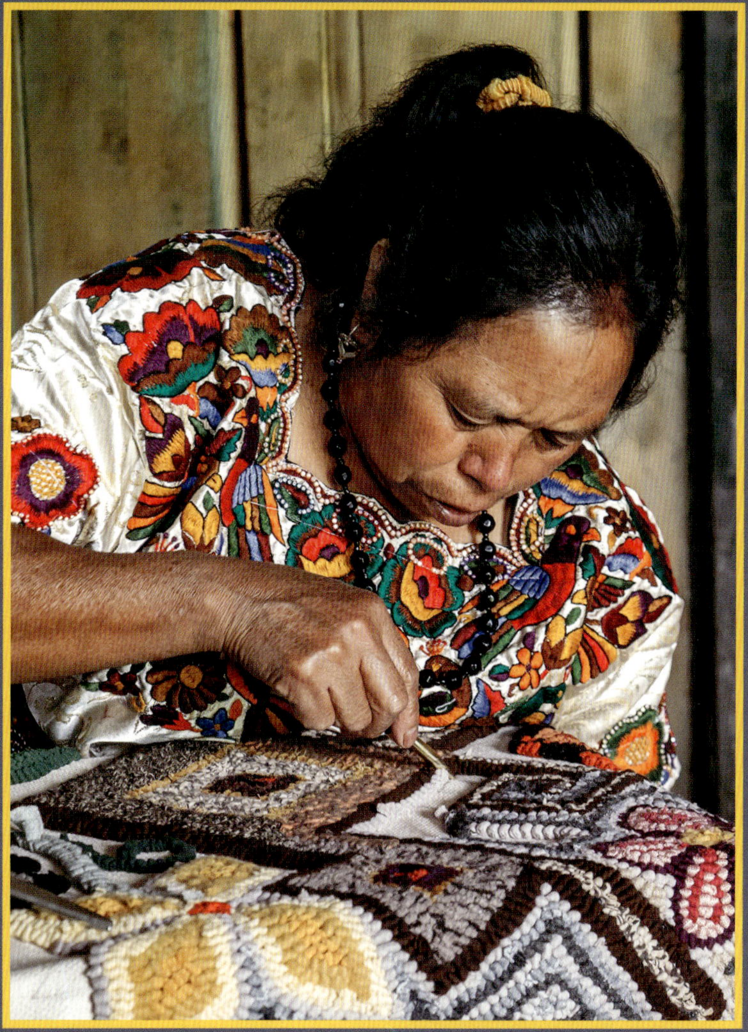
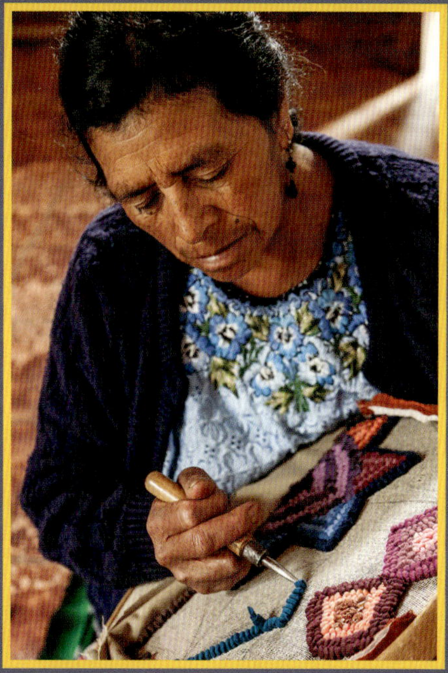
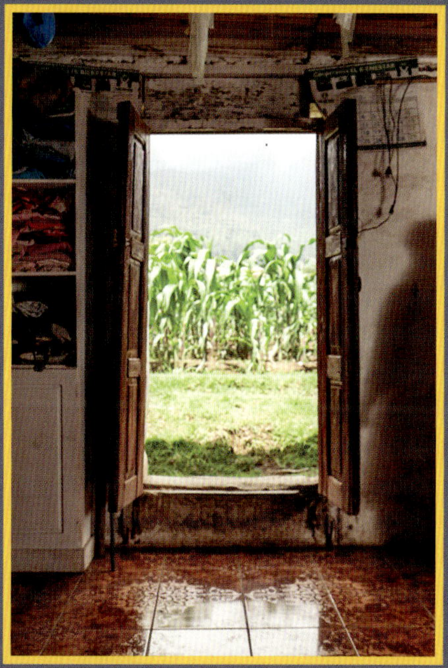
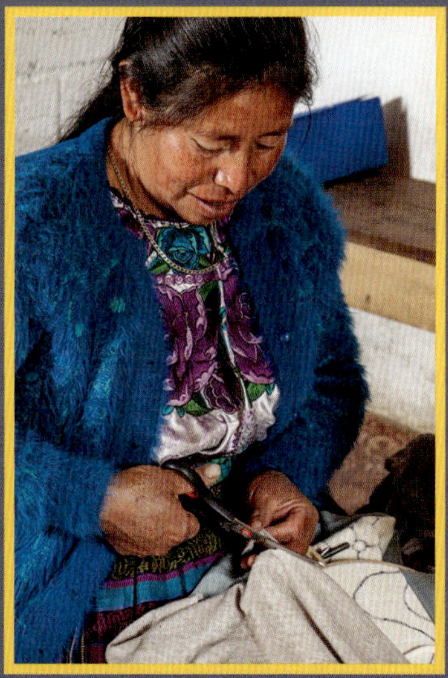
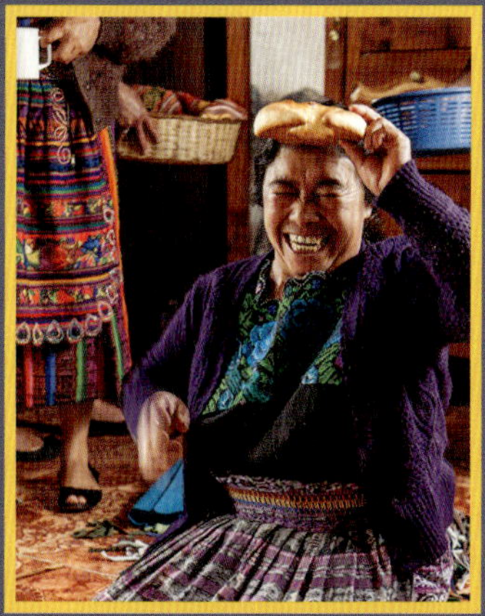

» Artists of the Chuacruz Rug-Hooking Group

LEFT TO RIGHT: Micaela, Yolanda, and Irma.

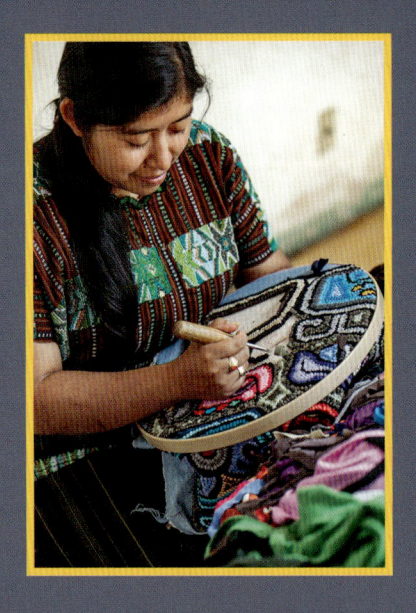

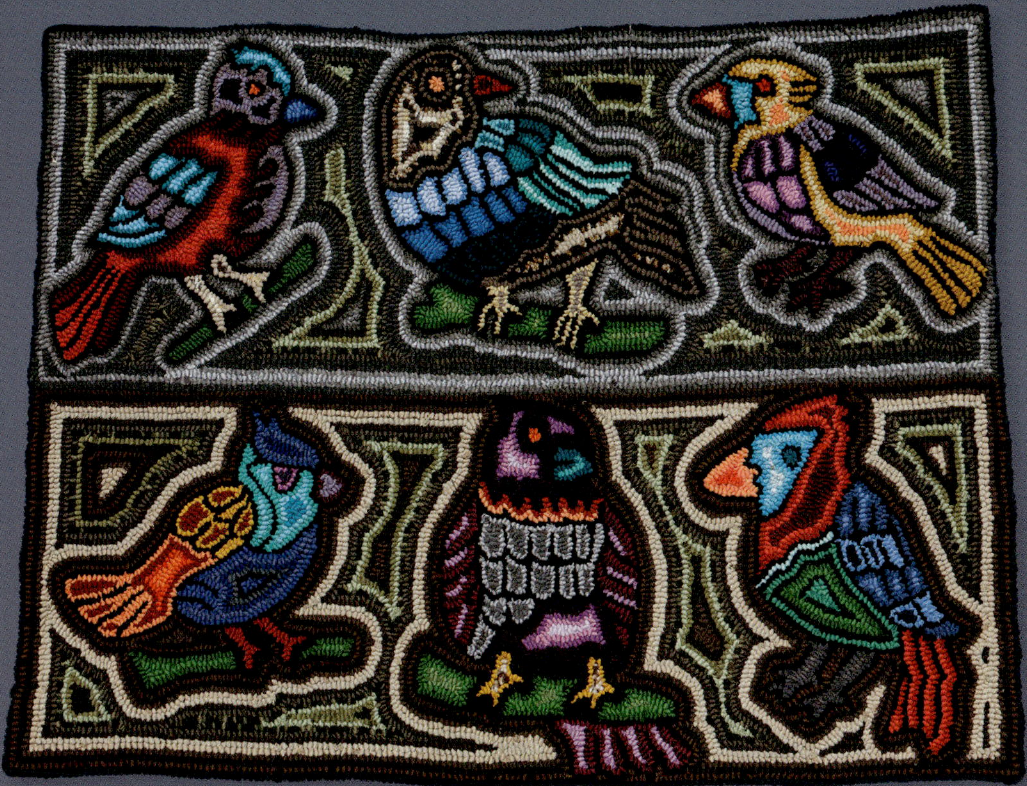

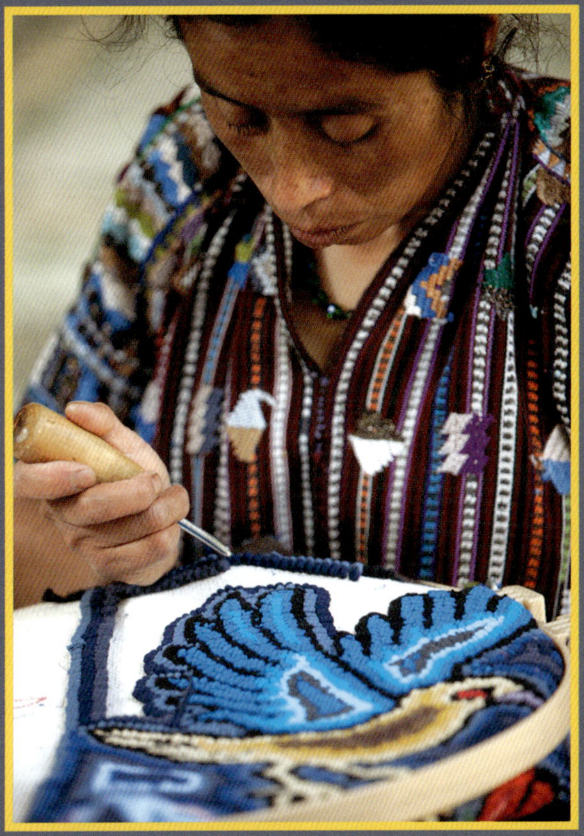

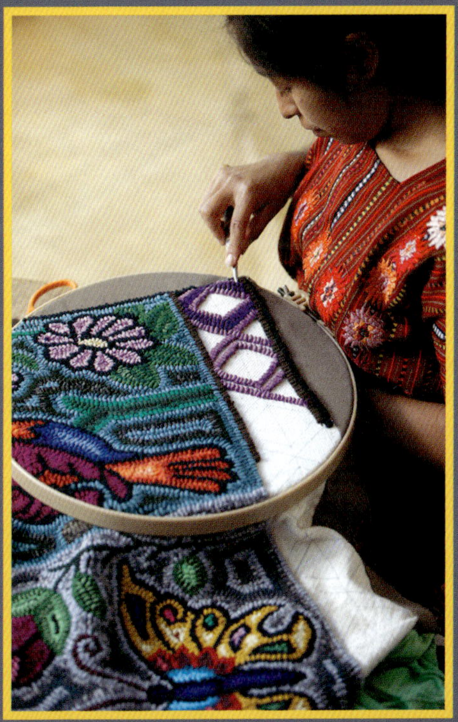

Part III:
Colors of the Future

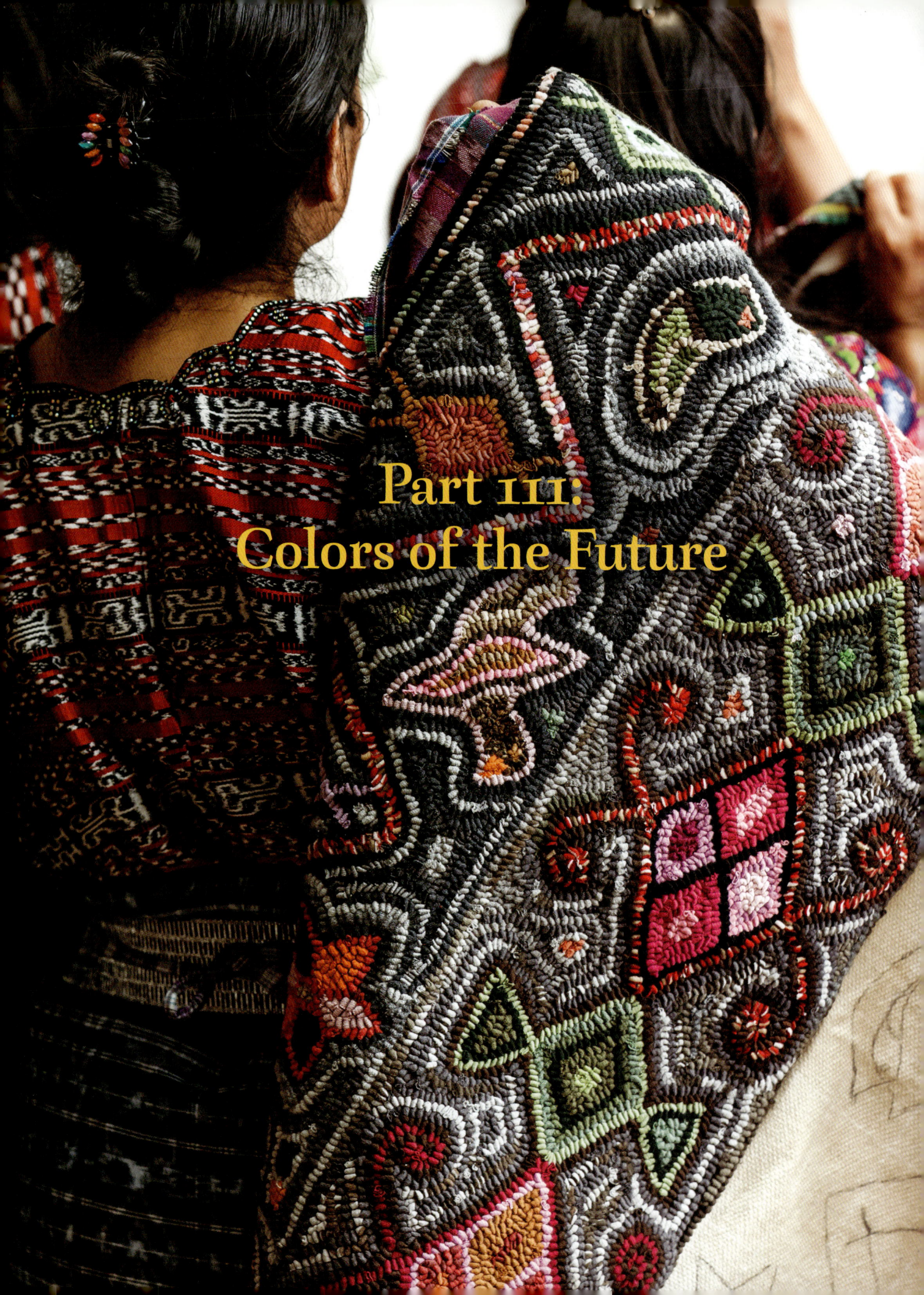

Multicolores: The New Organization Emerges
» Panajachel, Guatemala, 2014

In Multicolores's important first year as an independent nonprofit, Reyna and Cheryl, as a two-woman team, established procedures and systems and applied them to everything from accounting practices to communications. They designed systems for quality control, timely rug deliveries, transparent payment procedures, and more. Acceptance to the International Folk Art Market added a sense of urgency to their tasks. It also meant more visits to the communities to convey what the IFAM opportunity meant and to motivate the artisans to meet the Market's deadline. Reyna and Cheryl also created promotional materials and a budget and mapped out a calendar for the important foundational year ahead.

Following its successful debut at the Market, Multicolores also had the funds to train more women and expand the opportunity for participation in the rug-hooking program. Multicolores's first year had sped by and as more women came into the program, visits to the communities to meet the artisans in their home environments increased.

For a top-quality 2-by-4-foot rug, Multicolores pays the artist Q816 (about $110.) When this rug sells at retail for $375 at events like the IFAM, or at the Multicolores office or trunk show fundraisers, all proceeds (minus shipping, marketing materials, and travel expenses) are returned to Multicolores. The women receive a bonus of 30 percent or Q244.80 ($32.97). The balance of the funds help sustain Multicolores and implement new programs for artisans.

Envisioning a Larger Canvas
» Multicolores Office, Panajachel; Guatemala Highlands, 2015

Just as the artists made treks by foot and *microbus* (minitruck) from their homes to the highway, and then multiple bus transfers to Multicolores's office, Reyna and Cheryl took the same route, in reverse, to meet the women. While in the villages, they met the women's families and saw the living conditions where the artists worked at rug hooking. As their relationships strengthened, it was clear that Reyna and Cheryl had become like threads woven into the women's lives. Through their constancy, trust was built and barriers were dropped.

Opposite: Rosario prepares to show her rug to her compañeras in the Totonicapán rug-hooking group. ABOVE: A "chicken bus" bound for Panajachel.

Colors of the Future 103

During conversations with the artists, they heard comments about how participation in the program had affected the women. Rosa, a young woman from an impoverished family living in remote Quiejel, told how the experience of earning money had affected her relationship with her mother. *I have been able to acquire new knowledge, and at the same time to have income; never before did I have a Q100 bill ($13.50) to hold in my hand, my own money. I have to continue moving forward. My mother has given me more liberty so I can be part of the group and keep making rugs. My mother will tell me, "Leave the housework; I will do it." And when I come home from delivering rugs to the office, my mother will meet me by the roadside (highway) so that I don't have to walk back alone.*

Roxana, a woman in her thirties, tells her story:

I began to see life differently when I entered the rug-hooking project. Without a doubt, rug hooking has improved my family's quality of life. I consider myself an enterprising mother. I use part of the income from the sale of my rugs to ensure that my children have their basic needs met and the rest I invest in their education so that they can have a better future. The income also helps to cover household expenses: food, maintenance, and the other needs that arise. It is a help to my husband. I refer to my rug making as a team effort. My husband will often stop at the paca store to buy secondhand clothing; sometimes he helps me to cut the material into strips. My daughter, twelve, often helps with household chores or she will look after the two younger ones. My family supports me because they value my work and they can see that the additional income has helped our family situation. Working as a rug-hooking artist has changed my life. My self-esteem has improved. I feel more content because I feel valued as an artist and as a mother. I am proud that my family is involved in my work and can see the potential in me, and an example that no barriers exist to achieving new triumphs and successes in life. As a mother, I fight every day for the welfare of my family.

Irma was another young woman fighting for the chance to participate in the project. *When I first started in the rug-hooking project, I had no money to invest in paca, so I decided to use my husband's tee shirts. He looked for his shirts one day and couldn't find them, so pointing at my rug, I had to tell him I'd taken his tee shirts. I told him when my rug sold I would buy others for him. He didn't say anything, but you know, love makes you do crazy things; I think he forgave me.* By the time her rug was completed and sold, he had replaced his tee shirts. So instead of buying more tee shirts, she surprised him with a new pair of sports shoes.

A family of rug hookers (left to right) sisters Silvia, Yolanda, and Yessika Calgua.

Multicolores was gaining recognition. In the spring of 2015, the Avenir Museum, located on the campus of Colorado State University in Fort Collins, invited the artists to present an exhibition. The upcoming exhibit, which opened January 2016, would focus on large-format hooked rugs because the large rugs had an undeniable presence. Recognizing this fact, the exhibit's goal was to engage the museum-goers with the power of Maya women's artistry. A few months later, a similar exhibition was produced at the Textile Center in Minneapolis, Minnesota.

Aware that significant milestones are almost never documented, Jody and I bought the rugs exhibited at the Anderson Center from OB because we wanted a permanent collection to mark that milestone. Three rugs from that collection— by Yessika, Carmen, and Zoila—had gone to the Textile Museum of Canada in Toronto to be part of its 2013 exhibition, *Ancestry and Artistry, Maya Textiles from Guatemala*. The exhibition toured Canada for a year in 2014 and 2015.

In April 2015, Reyna and Yolanda Calgua Morales, were invited by network Channel 7 in Guatemala to appear on *Our World in the Morning* to talk about "The Rug Hooking Project: From Rags To Rugs!" During the live interview, Yolanda and Reyna told the story of how a group of motivated Maya women transformed their lives through rug hooking.

Rug-hooking artists whose work was featured in the Avenir Museum exhibition in 2016.
BELOW: Yolanda and Reyna on the set of *Our World in the Morning*.

Colors of the Future 105

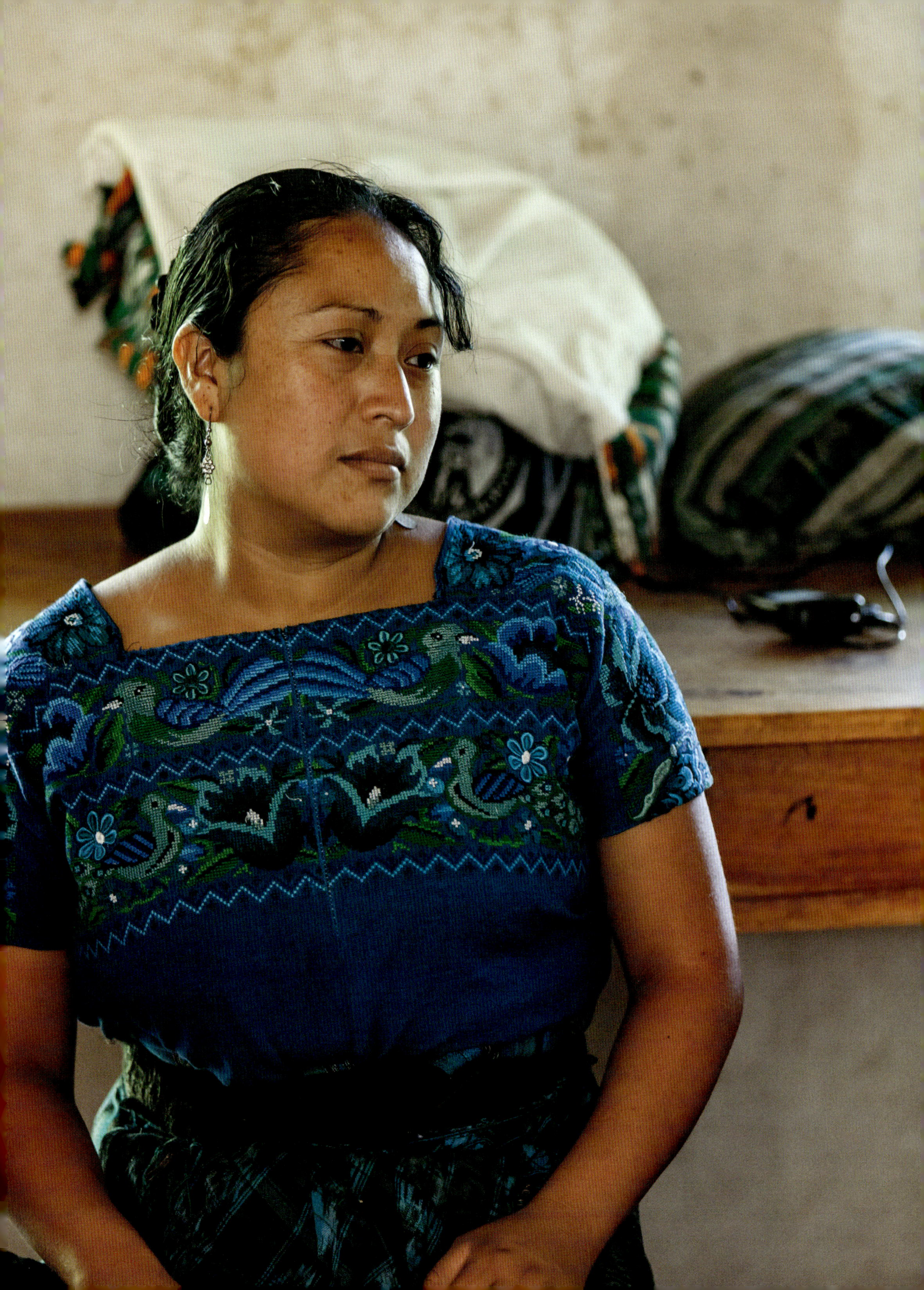

"My life has changed"
» Bartola Morales Tol, 28, San Jorge La Laguna

On being referred to as an artist, Bartola says, "When I hear you use the word 'artist' about me, it elevates me. I don't have the words to say what this signifies, but I am very happy. When people look at my rug, I want them to see the happiness, the emotion, the time that I have dedicated to it. They are seeing a part of me, and they will also see something from Guatemala. I seek inspiration in things that make me feel happy, like birds, flowers, and nature. The past has left many scars, but I keep moving forward to continue growing as an artist, mother, and wife."

In 2014, after becoming pregnant and wanting to find a way to earn money working at home, she approached Glendy, her cousin's wife, and asked to join the rug-hooking project. Working alongside of Glendy, Bartola discovered she possessed a natural aptitude for rug hooking. At first, she asked her husband to draw her designs because his drawing skill was better than hers. But she soon realized that she couldn't always rely upon him, and that with practice, she could learn to draw. Little by little, her drawing skill improved. She now enjoys a growing collection of templates, explaining, "The templates are like a catalog of design ideas I have created from my drawings." Continuing, she added, "My husband is very supportive of me. He knows what colors I like and what fabrics I use for my rugs, and sometimes on his way home from work, he will stop and buy me a bag full of paca. If I feel uncertain, I will ask his opinion about a color to use in my rug, and he always has a good idea for me."

Life was not always so agreeable. Bartola grew up feeling undermined by a father who directed most of his anger toward her, although, referring to her siblings, she says, "All of us were beaten." She still remembers his scathing comment when she asked to attend high school. "What's the point?" he replied. "You'll never make anything of your life; you'll soon swap carrying a backpack for carrying a baby." She completed the sixth grade and wanted to study more, but he insisted that she now work to help support the family. At age eleven, he sent her to work in a local canteen.

Bartola now lives with her husband and young daughter in San Jorge La Laguna, a hillside community overlooking Lake Atitlán. Three of his siblings, along with their children, share the small, dark house. Each family is confined to a single room. During the rainy season, they navigate rivulets of water that course through their dwelling. But Bartola anticipates better living conditions soon. Combining income from the sale of her rugs, her husband's salary, and a loan, the couple is adding on to the second level of his family's home and building their own apartment. She looks forward to the day she can move upstairs into the dry, bright new rooms, and have her own kitchen, too. When describing the new rooms, she adds, "I want to purchase a set of the rug-hooking furniture, (see page 123) like my compañeras have bought. But I have to wait for our rooms to be finished."

108   Bartola Morales Tol

I asked Bartola if there was anything she wanted to say to our readers.

"I'm not going to tell you I'm a strong woman, but I've learned a lot from what happened to me. These things left me with many scars, many wounds, but I am still here. I continue ahead, I won't let these things kill me, even though I was at the point of falling. The words of those who talk against me, they are only words, they can't affect me anymore." She went on to say, "I am succeeding as a rug-hooking artist, yet I still value the opinion of my teacher Glendy and my compañeras, too. When I finish a rug, I am eager to show it to them, to hear their opinion. I always want to improve. When I think about my rug being in a museum in Los Estados Unidos, I grow emotional." In 2016, Bartola's rug was one of six large-format hooked rugs included in the exhibition at the Textile Center in Minneapolis. "I wish I could have been in that room where my rug was on display. I imagine the feeling of seeing my rug in that room." She finished by describing her life with Multicolores, "I am happy, and I feel proud of myself because I know I am capable of doing more, of continuing to produce for Multicolores. My life has changed. I discovered a talent I never knew I had. I feel positive and self-confident. I no longer have to conform to my father's view of me."

Bartola Morales Tol 109

Reyna and Cheryl represent Multicolores at the Alliance for Artisan Enterprise competition in Washington, D.C. BELOW: Tomasa, María Sacalxot, and María Ignacia practice hand exercises they learned from Ann Fox.

In the summer of 2015, Multicolores and 150 artisans from 42 countries submitted entries to the Alliance for Artisan Enterprise's "Multimedia Competition." The competition featured stories and visual content that captured the value and impact of artisan enterprises worldwide. Multicolores was one of fifteen finalists shortlisted by the U.S. State Department's Office of Global Women's Issues and the Aspen Institute's Alliance for Artisan Enterprise competition. The rug-hooking project was recognized for its "creativity, resilience, and entrepreneurial spirit." In September, Reyna and Cheryl were flown to Washington, D.C. They joined their peers in the craft development field, policy makers, business leaders, and others in an event to celebrate the value and impact of the worldwide artisan sector.

Recognition for the women's artistry and hard work felt satisfying. But increasingly, Reyna and Cheryl envisioned a larger canvas for the scope of Multicolores's efforts. They had become motivated by the strength of their relationships with the women and by what they had witnessed and talked about, through long conversations held during their many visits in the communities.

That fall, the first workshop to address the physical needs of the artists was conducted by Ann Fox, a nurse from Minnesota. Ann had learned that some of the artists were complaining of sore wrists. She suspected they might be suffering from carpal tunnel syndrome. While in Guatemala on a volunteer nursing trip, she offered to conduct a hand-health workshop. She examined hands and brought along splints and gave instructions for how to apply them, cautioning the women to modify the hours they hooked each day. She also taught hand-health exercises that are now practiced in the rug-hooking communities.

Bringing the Men Along
» Multicolores Office, Panajachel; Guatemala Highlands, 2016

Throughout the year, stories emerged of husbands whose attitudes toward their wives were changing. When visiting the office one day, Glendy, wearing a mischievous smile, recalled how her husband had changed his attitude toward her rug making. She explained that her husband initially felt skeptical that her time spent rug hooking would result in income. And so, not wanting to antagonize him, in the afternoon while he was at work, she enlisted the help of their oldest daughter to prepare the evening meal. This reprieve gave Glendy a couple of hours each day to work at rug hooking. Then, late in the day, just before he arrived home from work, she would rush into the kitchen and make a show of banging around pots and pans as though she had been cooking for hours. As Glendy's rugs sold, her husband saw the obvious results of her labor. He realized that her rug making had a positive benefit for their entire family. To her satisfaction, he began to offer to clean the house and watch their toddler. His assistance opened more space for Glendy to hook rugs. Today, as coparents, they require that the older children help with cooking, cleaning, and supervising their younger siblings. Glendy says, "Now that I have this work, my children have become more responsible."

María Ignacia's husband was ambivalent about her participation. But after two years of consistently presenting him with income from rug money, he gave her a new, upgraded cell phone that had a camera. She recalls the day with pride. *I told him how my compañeras were able to use their cell phone cameras to document their rugs and how they also photographed things like huipils for design inspiration. I wasn't complaining to him, I was just describing how my compañeras kept a portfolio on their phone and I kept these ideas in my head. Not too long afterward, he gave me a phone with a camera. He didn't say much, but his gift means he is supporting me. I feel good about that.*

Maricela told her story, offering yet another example of husbands whose attitudes toward their wives had changed. She recalls learning about the project, admiring the rugs, and wanting to join Yolanda's rug-hooking group and learn the technique. But her husband wouldn't give his permission. Maricela was fortunate in one regard: Yolanda was her sister-in-law. Learning that Maricela's husband—Yolanda's brother—had refused his permission, Yolanda appeared at their house to have a talk with him. He soon changed his mind. In no time he was taking care of the children, enabling Maricela to participate in Multicolores workshops. Seeing the obvious results of her labor and admiring her artistry, he offered to help prepare her paca, too. Smiling and shaking her head at the memory, Maricela said,

As the Multicolores artists changed their perceptions of themselves, it spurred a change in the behavior of the men in their lives as well.

Colors of the Future

"I don't know what was wrong with him, but he couldn't cut the paca straight. I had to make him practice over and over. He finally learned how to cut the fabric, and now he is a big help to me."

Hilda's story is uncommon in that she had the full support from Catarina, her mother-in-law. Indeed, Catarina became an ally. She suggested that Hilda join her rug-hooking group, declaring, "You should learn to hook rugs, you don't want to be dependent on your husband all your life! What if he gets sick?" But Hilda's husband didn't think it was necessary for her to work. Watching her mother-in-law succeed at rug making, Hilda grew determined. Knowing her mother-in-law supported her, each morning when her husband left for work she began to learn rug making. Returning home, he didn't say much, and Hilda guessed it was because he saw that she was not neglecting her responsibilities for the children or household. She had a good relationship with him, and she wanted his feedback on her rugs, but he seldom commented on her artistry. Then one day, after returning home from participating in a workshop, Hilda remembered a tip Mary Anne had given the students about engaging family members in conversations about their artistry. Mary Anne said, "When someone gives you a compliment, thank them, maybe give them a genuine compliment back, or even a little piece of candy for their kind remarks." Recalling the suggestion, the next time Hilda's husband gave her a compliment on her rug, she reached into her apron's pocket and extracted a piece of chocolate, his favorite. She continued this gesture for a month. One day, her husband saw her latest rug and breaking into a proud, wide smile, he said, "This is beautiful! I never realized you had this talent!" Hilda thanked him, and reaching to embrace him, she gave him two pieces of chocolate.

Perhaps less dramatic, Silvia's story is nonetheless significant because through participating in the project and becoming an artist, she grew a sense of "personal space." From the moment she started rug hooking, she said, "My husband encouraged me and gave me permission to attend workshops at Multicolores. He saw that with my labor, we could have more money to support our family." Articulating a shift in the quality of her interior life, Silvia said, "For the first time ever, I feel like I am moving forward with my life. In doing this work, I get a chance to clear my mind."

Hearing comments like these helped Cheryl and Reyna understand that a change was occurring within the women. It appeared that mastering the craft and learning to become artists capable of success in the marketplace had triggered a subtle shift. The shift had ripple effects extending into the artists' families, too. Speaking about their artistry in voices of quiet surprise, one woman after another said, "I never knew I had this in me." Their statements of self-discovery seemed layered, textured, and complex.

With the encouragement of her mother-in-law, Hilda learned to hook rugs from her sister-in-law Ramona Tzunun. Now a highly accomplished artist, Hilda enjoys a new financial stability and growing self-confidence. OPPOSITE ABOVE: A rug by Irma Churunel features *nahuales*, traditional Maya birth symbols (see page 130). OPPOSITE BELOW: Nicolasa (left) and Pasquala (right) enjoy a moment together during a workshop at the Multicolores office.

Reyna and Cheryl were able to place the women's statements of self-discovery into context because some of the women had confided their personal histories. Some of the achievements, they knew, were hard won. They had learned that many of the women had left school at age eleven or younger to help support their families. Others had experienced years of parental neglect, attributable to the crippling effects of family alcoholism. Some of the women were victims of emotional abuse, rape, or incest. And so, just as the women had unearthed their artistry, Reyna and Cheryl began to dig for what these statements of self-discovery meant. They resolved to learn how to support the women to achieve even more.

Colors of the Future   113

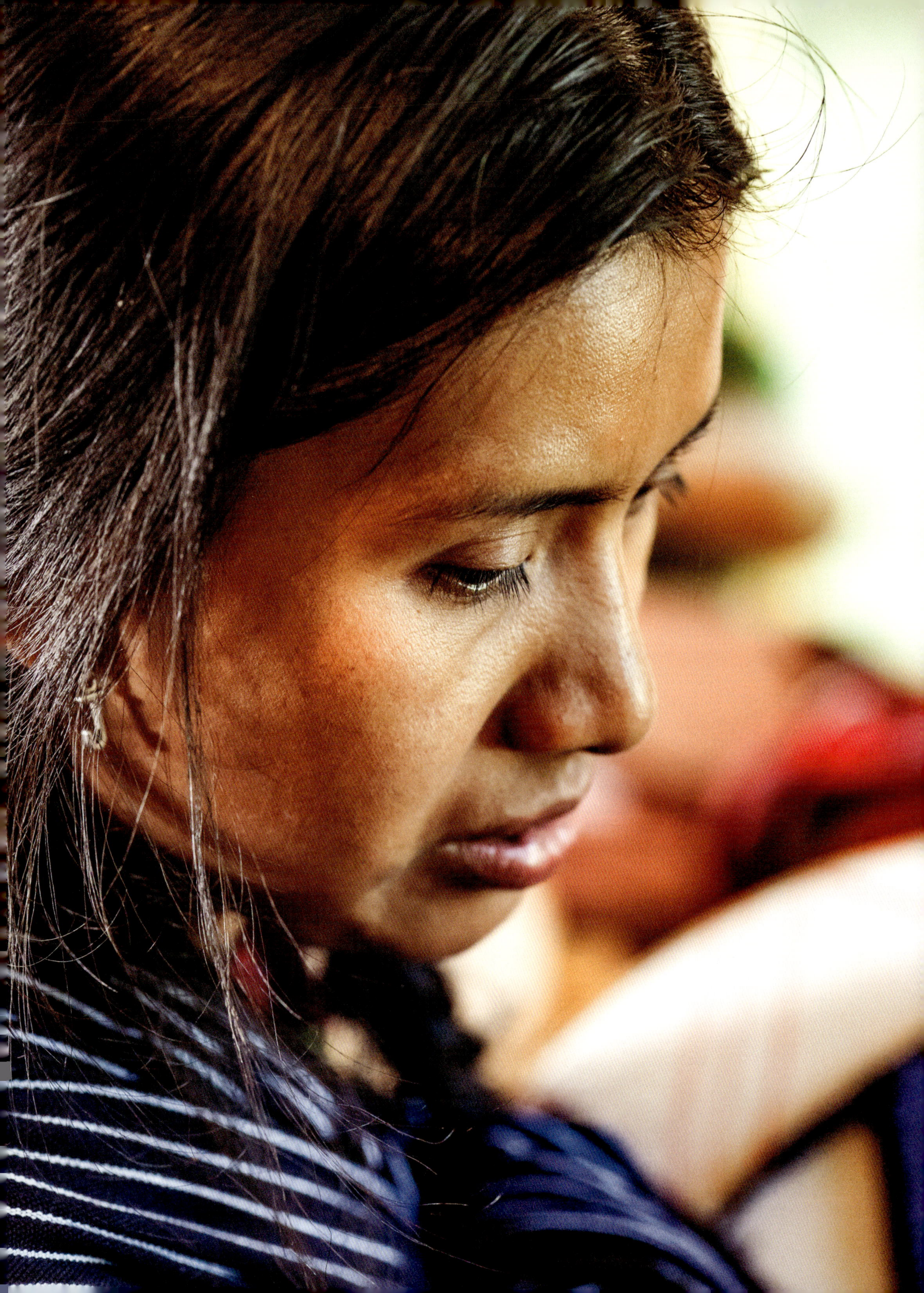

"The changes I have gone through are many"
» Juana Calel Yax de Gonzalex, 28, Patanatic

Among Juana's seventeen siblings, their mother's courage is legendary. Her father was abusive and her mother would protect the children from his angry tirades. Only her brothers were allowed to attend school because her father believed that sending girls to school was a waste of money and time. As the youngest girl, Juana was expected to serve the family, to cook and clean up after them. Food was scarce. If she took too large a portion or spilled the corn or burned the tortillas, she was beaten. To escape this abusive environment, Juana married at age seventeen.

The newlyweds put money down to buy a small plot of land where they dreamed of building a home one day. The home would provide stability for their family. Her husband was employed driving a microbus, but Juana's options for work were limited. There was never enough money. The family frequently moved, always hoping to find a situation they could afford while paying off the land. When Juana lost her job working for a street vendor who sold snacks, the family became homeless. She tried to sell her embroidery, going shop to shop in a nearby town, but the sporadic sales weren't sufficient.

Desperate for work, one day Juana ran into Glendy, an acquaintance from her village. She had heard of Glendy's work in the rug-hooking project, and she knew Glendy to be a kind and thoughtful person. And so she approached Glendy and explained her desperate situation. Feeling as if she had nothing to lose, she forthrightly asked to join her group. Glendy said yes.

Juana expresses her gratitude for Glendy's kindness:
New members usually have to hook a small sample to see if their skill has promise. But Glendy understood I was desperate. She could see I was determined. I could embroider, and I could sew, and I was determined to learn this work, too. So she didn't make me first hook a sample; she gave me a big piece of ground cloth and all the paca I needed to finish the rug. She sat with me all day and helped me. I came back to her house every day until my rug was done. Then one morning, I went with Glendy to the Multicolores office to deliver my rug. Glendy explained that if my rug quality was good, I would get paid right away. All I could think about was how badly my family needed the money. So this was an important day. But my rug had many problems. Reyna was there, and I think she also knew how desperate my situation had become. Reyna stayed with me and told me how I needed to change my rug if I wanted to get paid. She did not abandon me, and I am very grateful for her patience. I did the changes she suggested and doing those changes, I learned a lot in a short time. When I finally finished, Reyna paid me. It was very late in the day, after dark, when I came home with my first rug money. But it was a good feeling; that memory will stay with me for a long time.

Using income from her husband's job and Juana's steady rug money, the family was able to build a two-room home on their land. They bought a stove and one day Juana hopes to add a third room, a kitchen, where she can possibly have a water tap, too. Their lives are improving, they bought a second bed where the children now sleep, and Juana bought a sewing machine to expand her capacity for work.

Juana Calel Yax de Gonzalex

"My husband supports my working; he always has. He sometimes says to me, 'Thank God you were willing to marry me—you are such a hard worker!' He will help me cut my paca, and if we need the money to pay a bill, and if my rug is almost done, he will hire my sister to wash our clothes or help with the cooking so I can finish my rug, deliver it, and get paid."

Juana credits Multicolores for her improved circumstances. "When I first met Glendy, I didn't speak much Spanish. I grew up speaking K'iche' and now, through attending workshops at Multicolores and being on the tours, my Spanish has greatly improved. This is the first time I've participated in a group with other women, and the changes I have gone through are many. We support one another, and if a new person comes into our group, I can help them. I can help them draw their designs because drawing is a skill I didn't know I had until I started this work." Smiling shyly at me and lowering her voice, she adds, "I've become good at drawing. I go right from my idea to drawing the design on my ground cloth. I don't need to use templates because I can draw my ideas."

When asked where her rug design ideas come from, Juana said, "They are everywhere." Continuing, she confides, "Sometimes when I am in Pana I might see a woman wearing a beautiful huipil or *faja* (belt), and I will follow her in secret for a little while to get a better look. I am able to remember those designs, and I put them in my rugs."

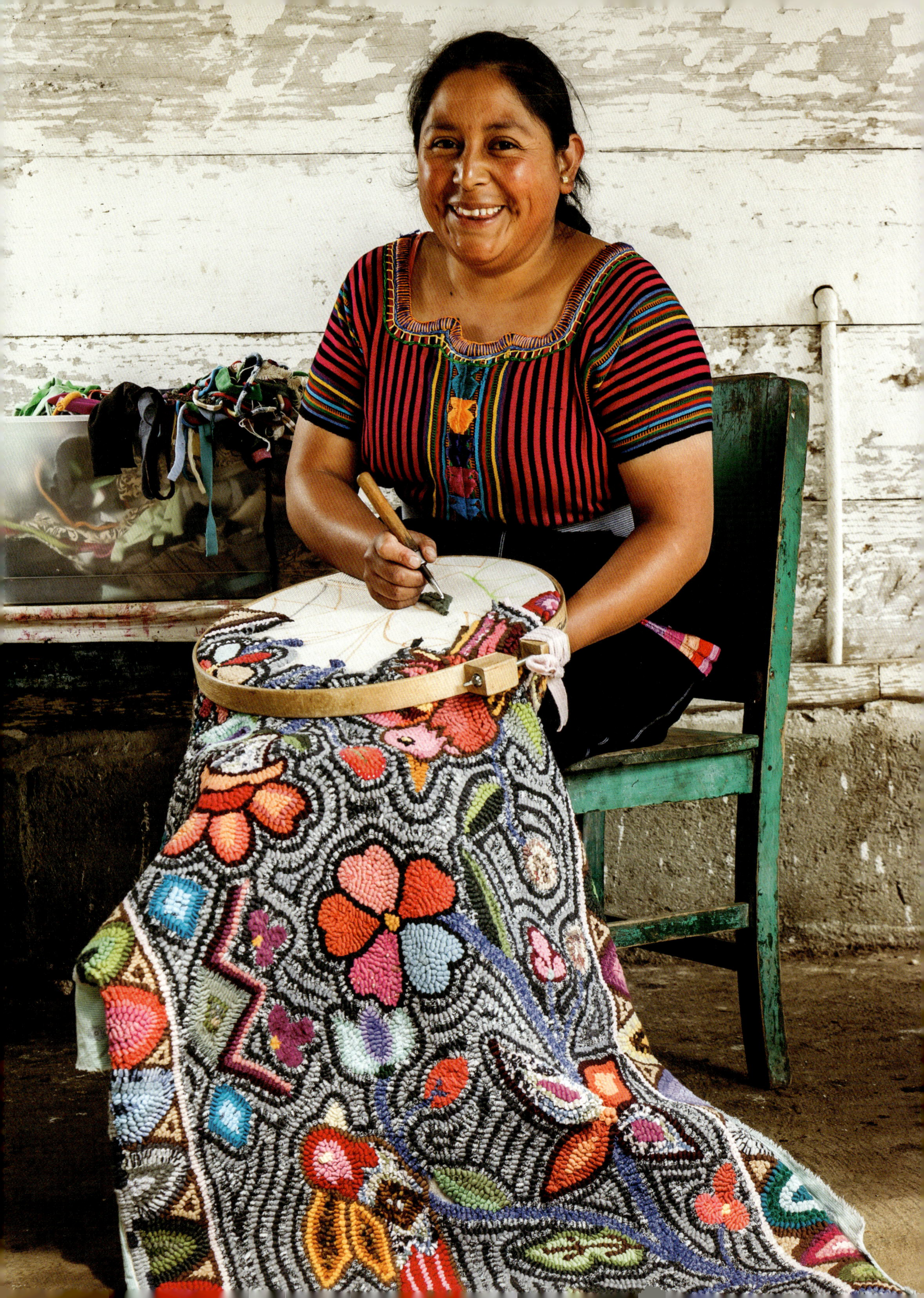

"I am learning to start living without regrets"
» María Ignacia Vicente Jocol, 29, Chirijquaic

María Ignacia lives in the rural village of Chirijquaic in the western highlands of Guatemala, with her husband and two children, a son aged eleven and a daughter aged five. She attended school until the sixth grade. Her husband, thirty-six, works as an attendant at a gasoline station. She married at seventeen.

Chirijquaic has a population of less than 1,000 inhabitants and is mainly an agricultural area. Like many families in her village, María Ignacia cultivates corn and beans on a small plot of land close to her home. She also raises chickens. Alongside rug hooking, María Ignacia is a skilled weaver and embroiderer, and she also ties *jaspe* (ikat) for *corte* (skirts).

María Ignacia learned to hook rugs in 2013. She found the technique difficult in the beginning and pays tribute to roving rug-hooking teacher Yolanda Calgua Morales, who taught classes in her community, for encouraging her not to give up and always motivating her with "You can do it!" With income from rug hooking, she can buy things for her home, buy more food for the family, have healthcare.

On the path to becoming a skilled rug hooker, María Ignacia has had to overcome many difficulties. In the beginning, her husband did not give her permission to attend workshops at the Multicolores office in Panajachel, but after hooking two large rugs and earning significant income, he saw the benefits and has become much more supportive of her and her work.

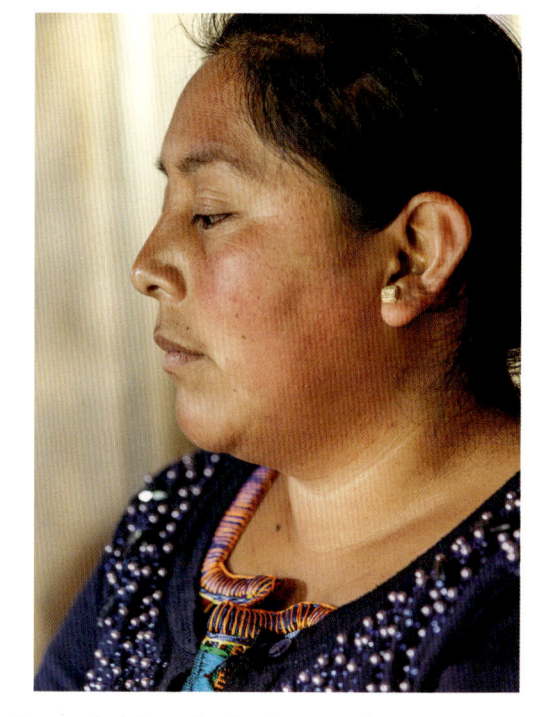

She no longer has to ask his permission to attend workshops. María Ignacia commented, "Women have to ask their husbands for permission to have dreams," meaning that their lives are limited by what their husbands permit. But being part of Multicolores and the rug-hooking project has changed the way she sees herself. She feels stronger, more determined; she expresses herself and makes her own decisions. It wasn't always so!

María Ignacia suffered as a child. Her father died when she was three and her mother, unable to cope, turned to alcohol. María Ignacia has grown up without much family support which continues to this day. However, in Multicolores, she has found her family, saying, "I know I have a family apart from my own family. I have Multicolores. I am always excited when I go there; everyone is always happy to see me, encouraging me, asking how I am. We are all united as a group." Through workshops and through being part of Multicolores, her world has expanded, and she has been able to travel outside her small rural village.

María Ignacia describes herself as a woman who overcomes: "Multicolores lifted me from where I was…mourning the loss of a child, depressed, going through a difficult time with my husband and mother. But through the workshops I learned something important; if I wanted to overcome something I could, that if I put my mind to something, I could do it. I am learning to start living without regrets."

Maria Ignacia Vicente Jocol   121

Aura Perez Can, Social Services Coordinator for Multicolores. Her work with the rug-hooking artists has taught her, "As human beings, we have no boundaries."

To define new goals for the women, and to reach them, Reyna and Cheryl needed help. They turned to Aura Marina Perez Can, a social worker who grew up in Panajachel. Reyna and Cheryl interviewed and hired Aura as the Social Service Coordinator in December 2015, and she began work in January 2016. Speaking about the opportunity to join Multicolores and help shape the agenda, Aura said: *Women and girls in Guatemala have been affected by limited opportunities since a very young age. Opportunities to develop their own skills have often been neglected or denied to them. I visualize that Multicolores is contributing to social change in our country, bringing opportunities to our communities, specifically with women in their homes. I see that the women of Multicolores are changing; they are going beyond stereotypes and they are bringing the men along with them.*

To illustrate her point, Aura cites Gloria's hard work. Gloria said: *I wanted to be part of the project, to learn this work. I could see it was not as hard on my body as other work I have had. I dreamed of relying only on myself, of working at home. I could see how others in the group had accomplished that. But my husband was jealous and would not let me. Finally, my brothers-in-law talked to my husband; they helped convince him to let me try. He no longer threatens that he will go back to Los Estados Unidos for work; in fact, he helps me. He cuts my paca and helps me draw my design if I get frustrated. He sometimes suggests colors to use, and he supports me. His help motivates me, and he says "Yes!" when I ask to go to a Multicolores workshop because he wants me to learn more. Now that I am earning income from rug making, I feel more freedom, more useful, and I can buy what I want according to my own tastes. I want my daughter to learn this work because even though she is in school, there are very few jobs. If she has this work, she can rely on herself. The biggest change I have seen is to have gained the trust of my husband. Now there is more harmony at home, there is mutual sharing and support.*

Aura singles out yet another artist, Delores, for her bravery. Delores told Aura that her husband is frequently unemployed. His lack of employment motivated her to join her friend's rug-hooking group. Her husband didn't believe she could earn money rug hooking, but she soon presented him with money earned from the sale of her first rug. However, instead of celebrating her accomplishment, he became jealous. One day, while Delores was away from home, he opened the plastic bags containing her investment of paca for rug hooking and poured water in the bags, soaking the fabrics. By the time she discovered the mess, the cloth had mildewed and rotted. She confronted him, and holding her ground, told him she would not quit the project in spite of his feelings.

Continuing, Aura recalled another woman's story. "Calendaria's story is nuanced because it reveals not only how her relationship with her husband improved through her participation in this project, but also how she has grown more confidence."

Calendaria said: *I talk freely now, but before, I was scared to offer my opinion. Now I make my own purchasing decisions (because I have my own money); before, I had to ask my husband. Before, my husband was very jealous. I had to bring lunch to him every day where he worked. But now he thinks differently; he gives me more freedom to attend workshops at Multicolores. Now he buys his own food for lunch. I don't have to bring it to him.*

A Plan for Life

Reyna and Cheryl, and now Aura, began to envision programs to support the lives of the artists. The programs would be informed by ongoing participation of the artists and by what Reyna and Cheryl observed during their many visits in the communities.

One of their most lasting impressions was observing women at work rug hooking. It was evident that the women did not have places within their homes dedicated to making rugs. They learned that all the women but two owned a table and chair. However, in the homes of those who owned a table and chair, the furniture was commandeered by the entire family. For some of the rug hookers, the family bed became their workplace. With their rug hooking hoop or frame upon their lap and colorful strips of paca flowing across the hilly terrain of blankets and sheets, the artists leaned against the wall and worked on their rugs. Often, a baby or grandparent lay dozing in the bed beside them. Other artists sat on overturned buckets, or on a *petate* (thin reed mat) on the floor. They noted that all of the women, with two exceptions, had electricity, but most of the homes were dark and poorly lit. Some of the homes were a single room with one window and the bedroom was also the kitchen. Years of cooking fires had blackened the walls and light that filtered in from the window or doorway was quickly absorbed. In several of the homes, they observed that paca for rug hooking was hung from a web of rope strung about the room. Hanging their investment of paca kept it off the floor, safe from rats.

Homes nestled in the hillside near the community of Quiejel.

Among the priorities the team recommended was to offer the artists help in establishing better working conditions. Working with the artists, they assembled a list of furniture needs. The list included:

1. A sturdy wooden table
2. A sturdy, cushioned chair
3. A floor lamp with a bright bulb
4. Plastic bins to keep the cut paca strips organized
5. A sturdy wooden cupboard with cubbyholes to contain paca, one that has a compartment with a door that locks, affording the artist a place to keep certain belongings private and secure

Colors of the Future 123

The furniture would be offered first to the most productive artists and would be paid for through donations and by the artists, who would pay half the cost.

A rug-hooking tour participant, intent upon making a donation for furniture, asked Cheryl, "Why not donate the furniture, why make the women share the cost? It seems like a lot of money for them."

"The philosophy of cost-sharing is important in Multicolores," explained Cheryl. "We are not a paternalistic organization, nor do we want to create dependency, which is why we require the artists 'to put some skin in the game,' because it's empowering. We recognize that to be truly empowered, the women must be active participants in identifying the problems, the solutions, and the implementation strategies."

The artists would pay half the cost, $112.50. They could make payments over time, deducting their payment from rug money. Cheryl launched an online fundraising campaign and initially, seventeen women signed on to receive the furniture. The furniture project is ongoing, and any donations remaining from the campaign have been set aside to meet future requests.

On the day the furniture was delivered, the artists waited along the roadside eager for the sight of the delivery truck. Meeting the truck at the roadside was the first stop along the delivery route. Many of the women live off of the highway, along twisting footpaths that snake across farm fields or down narrow alleyways. Their homes are inaccessible by car or truck which meant the furniture would have to be carried the final leg. Anticipating the delivery, the women had cleared spaces in their homes. And now, finally, with the furniture in place, they savored the time spent organizing their paca, often by color.

In creating a space within their homes dedicated to rug hooking, their sense of accomplishment expanded, along with their self-worth. By choosing to spend scarce resources to create a comfortable and organized place to work, the women were affirming their value as artists within their families.

Nicolasa oversees the loading of her new cabinet bound for a prominent place in her home.

Building on the success of the furniture program, the team contemplated other ways they could support the women. But in order to ensure that any actions taken would be in line with what the women wanted and needed, they would first conduct a needs analysis—a way of asking a community or group what they consider to be their most important needs. It's used to supplement one's own observations and experience.

But how to conduct a thorough and systematic analysis became the question. Aura remembered participating in a *Planificación de Vida* (Life Plan) class in high school. This class helped Aura visualize a life beyond her circumstances, which at the time, were difficult. In recalling the class, Aura said, "Participating in that class had a profound impact on me. In fact, to this day, I will review my exercise book to determine if I am on track and I'm meeting the goals I set."

Aura and Reyna wondered if any of the women had ever participated in a Life Plan class, and decided the format was a good way to get to know the women's wants and needs. The methodology included such questions as Who am I? How do I see myself? What are my goals in life? What are my strengths? My weaknesses?

The Planificación de Vida workshop was held in November 2016. In speaking about the workshop results, Reyna and Aura felt inspired by what they had learned. Most of the women had never been asked to speak about their dreams. Yet as the daylong workshop unfolded, they heard the women give voice—and names— to their dreams. These included learning to drive, dancing, practicing yoga, finishing high school, seeing their children graduate, looking for scholarships for their children, learning English or Spanish, taking other courses, seeing the home of a person who purchased their rug, having their own home/land/car/domestic appliances/furniture, having savings, starting a business, medical checkups, and psychological help. They also wanted to learn how they could be more active in their communities, how to receive help to become better artisans and leaders, and how to learn about additional sources of income besides rug hooking.

During the workshop, some women exclaimed, "I had never thought about these questions. And now I see that it is so important to have goals because otherwise we only live day to day."

Glendy works in her studio at home. BELOW: An extraordinary rug hooked by Nicolasa Pacay illustrates proportion, master colorwork, and multidimensional design.

Colors of the Future   125

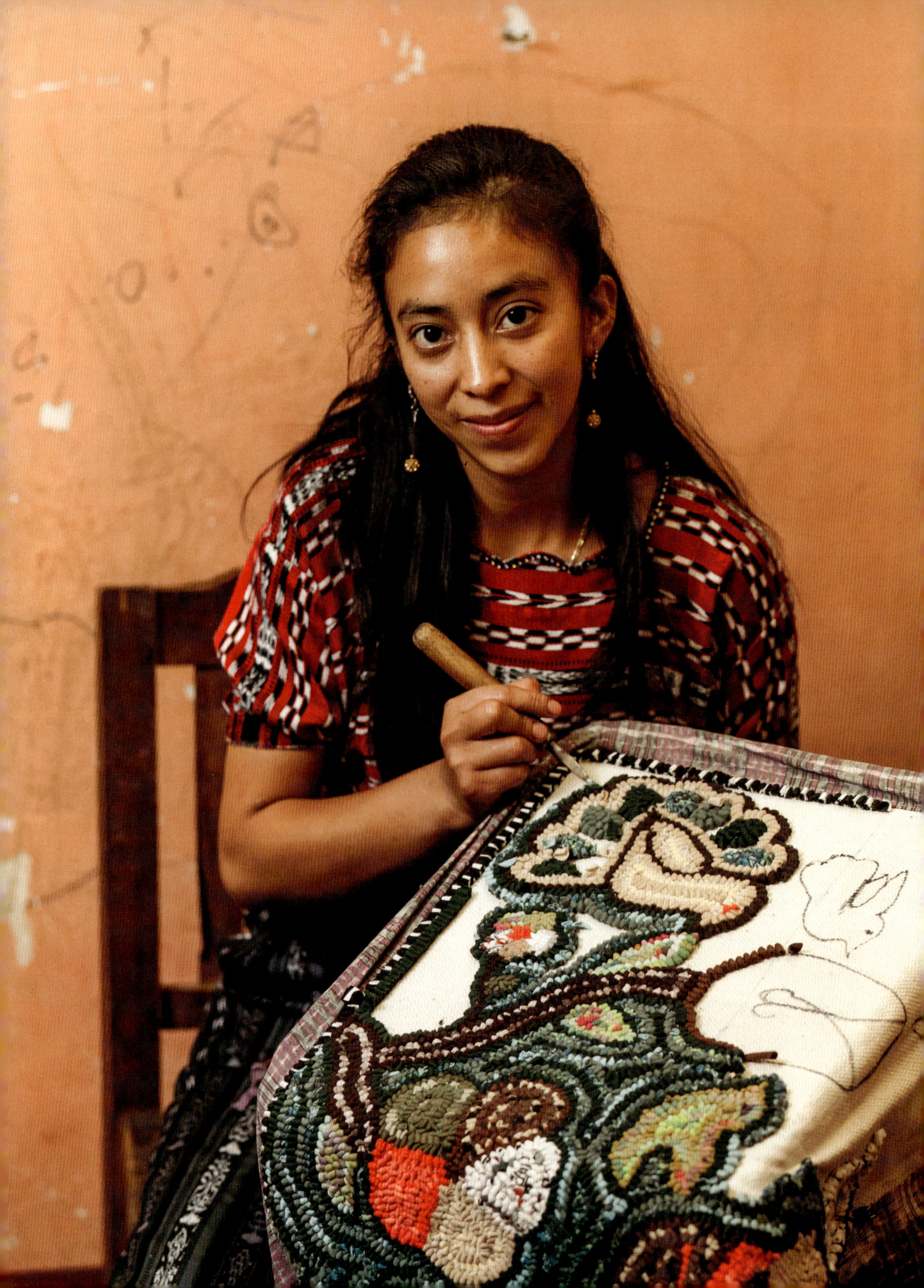

"Thank you for helping Maya Women"
» Hilda Raquel García Tzunun, 22, Chiyax

Hilda lives with her husband, who is a weaver, and their two children, a six-year-old girl and three-year-old boy, in the village of Chiyax, forty-five minutes from the city of Totonicapán, in the southwestern highlands of Guatemala. The population is 98 percent Maya K'iche' who speak K'iche'. Spanish is also spoken. In the village, farmers grow corn, apples, peaches, beans, potatoes, and pumpkins. Artisans embroider, make footwear, and weave using a foot loom. Hilda left school at fifteen, when she got married. One of her goals is to finish school.

Hilda learned rug hooking in 2012 from her sister-in-law, rug-hooking teacher Ramona Tzunun. Hilda calls herself an artist. For her, the name signifies loving what you do—what Hilda feels she transmits into her rugs. She likes the vitality she gives to her work. When she sees something that she likes, she keeps it in her mind, and when she gets home she draws it in her notebook. She keeps doing this until she has enough ideas to design her rug. Hilda uses income from rug hooking for food, clothing, and materials for house construction. She and her husband are in the process of building their own home.

In the beginning, Hilda's husband thought he could cover the household expenses; therefore, it wasn't necessary for her to work. During this time, Hilda's mother-in-law, who was a member of the Totonicapán Rug-Hooking Group, was a great ally and encouraged her to rug hook. Hilda started to work on her rugs in the morning when her husband was at work, and when her husband saw that she was able to earn money without neglecting her responsibilities at home, he gave permission for her to join the Totonicapán group.

Hilda is grateful for the opportunity that she has been given. If it wasn't for Multicolores, she wouldn't know the talent that she has. Being part

128   Hilda Raquel García Tzunun

of Multicolores and participating in workshops where she shares her views has really helped her self-confidence. Before, her husband didn't say very much to her; if something happened or he needed something, he told his mother and she told Hilda. She now trusts herself to solve problems in their marriage. They have a much better dialogue and a more equal relationship. Hilda teaches her children that life isn't always as they see it. It can be different. It can be better.

Hilda acknowledges Mary Anne, Reyna, and Cheryl, saying, "Thank you for helping Maya women. You have overcome many barriers that Multicolores has encountered. I would like to congratulate you and encourage you to keep moving forward. We hope that you don't falter or fall, but if you do, we are here to pick you up."

Hilda Raquel García Tzunun

Walter Amilcar Paz Joj teaching several rug hooking artists about nahuales to incorporate into their rug designs. Those artists who have attended school likely learned about the Mayan Calendar, but the value and traditions of nahuales are not taught, so they had limited knowledge of this powerful cultural symbol.

Toolbox for Life
» Multicolores Office, Panajachel, Guatemala, 2017

The team resolved to help the women achieve their goals. This would be accomplished through more integrated programming. The team would develop workshops to support the women's continued growth as artists, alongside programs to support their well-being. They acknowledged that the tools the rug hookers learned on their path to mastering the craft and becoming artists had provided foundational knowledge to grow more skills. They knew the women were extremely motivated and hard working. If the organization could design programs to expand the tools in their artists' toolboxes, and now learn tools for life, the women would have more opportunities. As an organization, they determined to be concerned for the women's welfare in all areas of their lives, not only where their lives intersected with Multicolores. The resulting holistic plan would be implemented in early 2017 with plans to continue for the next three years with periodic reviews and outside experts called upon when needed. In addition to skills honing the women's artistic abilities, additional workshops addressed concerns about time management, nutrition and health, and saving money.

Growing as Artists
Reyna recalled that recently when rug deliveries were made to the office, some of the women admired rugs made by certain artists who used *nahuales* (Maya birth

symbols) in their designs. She learned that many of the women did not know the cultural significance of nahuales and was determined to provide this information in a workshop taught by local expert and artist, Walter Amilcar Paz Joj. Understanding the significance of nahuales would expand the women's source of design.

During the Planificación de Vida workshop, Reyna remembered the comment made by a young artist who said she would like to see the home of someone who bought her rug. This gave Reyna an idea. She had been thinking about expanding the palette for rugs created for the IFAM, reasoning that an expanded palette, using neutral colors, for example, could increase their customer base. Further, the expanded palette could build upon information conveyed at a color workshop taught the previous year by Keith Recker, an expert on color. Reyna gathered home interior magazines and instructed the women to peruse the magazines and choose one of the featured rooms. Then she challenged the women to determine a palette for a rug that would coordinate with the room they had selected from the magazine. As the workshop concluded, the women began to grow an understanding of how U.S. interiors are put together and how to choose a palette of colors for a specific space.

Participants in Keith Recker's color workshop.

Colors of the Future

Time Management

In tandem with the color workshop was a workshop on time management. It was not a linear projection from a color workshop to time management. However, Reyna rightly concluded that if an artist felt more confident in her color choices, she would make better use of her time. While visiting the communities to teach the workshop, having opened the topic of time management skills for discussion, the women added surprising reasons for learning this skill. "My neighbor comes over and wants to talk every day; she will talk for hours. I can't hook with her sitting there; it is too hard to make design decisions with her in my room."

Hearing their comments, Reyna and Cheryl distributed a piece of paper printed with a 24-hour pie chart. They instructed the women to fill out the chart, making note of the activities they did within each hour of the day. Examining their completed charts, the women expressed surprise by how much time was taken up doing dishes, cooking, and other household chores. Added to some charts were the hours a neighbor came over to talk, or the time spent watching *novellas* (soap operas), or the time spent going to the market to buy food. Chatty neighbors, watching too much TV, and spending time shopping for food every day prompted further discussions. Reyna suggested, "Why not cut your paca while your neighbor sits talking with you? For those of you who have a TV, you don't have to stop watching your novellas. Use that time to cut paca or organize your colors. If you made a meal plan for the week and created a shopping list, you could probably go to the market only two or three times a week."

Maricela from the Quiejel rug-hooking group nearing completion of another rug.

Soon the discussion switched to center on wages earned from rug hooking. The women in the Chirijquiac and Totonicapán rug-hooking communities compared rug income to income earned through agricultural work. They reported that a man who is uneducated and unskilled, who is able to find work in agriculture, earns between Q75 and Q80 per day ($10.13 to $10.80). A woman in the same community and circumstance can earn Q40 per day ($5.40). Cheryl pointed out that the minimum wage is Q86.90 per day ($11.74). The women responded, all talking at once, voicing acknowledgment that "not many people earn the minimum wage around here." Reyna reminded them that if they hooked 12 by 12 inches in a day, or one square foot, they would earn Q102 per day ($13.78). She added, "This amount of money is more than the minimum wage."

Everyone loved the idea of earning so much money—but they immediately cited reasons why they could never accomplish this much hooking in a day. It was "too much to hook in a day because they didn't have their paca cut," or they "couldn't hook that much in a day because it took too long to decide what colors to use," and they "couldn't do their chores *and* that much hooking in a day, too." Hearing their doubts, Reyna quietly held up a 12-by-12-inch piece of paper. Judging by the looks on the women's faces, it was clear that none of them had taken the time to visualize what a "square foot" actually looked like. And suddenly, for some of the women, the notion of completing 12 by 12 inches of hooking in a day appeared like an achievable option. They sat up straighter and resumed the discussion of time management, meal planning, making grocery lists, how to deal with chatty neighbors, and more.

132 Colors of the Future

Nutrition Education

During a visit to the communities while conducting the time management workshops, Reyna and Cheryl compiled information about what the women ate for breakfast that day as well as the foods that would comprise their meals for the next few days. The answers solidified for the team the need to create awareness about the role diet plays in maintaining energetic bodies able to regulate metabolisms. The women expressed a desire to earn more income—so the question became how to expand awareness of the relationship between diet and energy. The role of diet and nutrition would fit with the topic of time management because maintaining energy is key to productivity. Further, both Reyna and Cheryl understood that improvements to the family's diet would promote healthier growth for their children.

This information was analyzed and followed up by a second workshop which outlined the fundamental objectives of nutrition: producing energy, regulating metabolism, enabling growth. The group also discussed what makes a good meal: fruits and vegetables, cereal and tubers, legumes, and foods of animal origin. And they learned what nutritional value each of those groups has: vitamins and minerals, fiber, protein, and so on.

Discussions ensued about how diets have changed from the days of their grandmothers. All the women seemed to recognize there are more candy, soft drinks, and chips in the diet now. Everyone seemed to recognize that these additions to their diets were not healthy habits. Everyone agreed to come up with an intercambio of recipes, and they agreed to request recipes from their grandmothers, in particular. They liked the idea of coming up with a week's worth of healthy choices that would be analyzed by a nutritionist. As the conversation grew and the women became excited about improvements to their diets, some suggested classes on creating organic gardens for their families. Future activities in the nutrition program include cooking lessons in the communities in which participants test a selection of the recipes.

A farmer works his fields near Chuacruz
BELOW: Maria Estela Az Tamayac combined figurative images with geometric elements in hooking this lively rug.

Colors of the Future

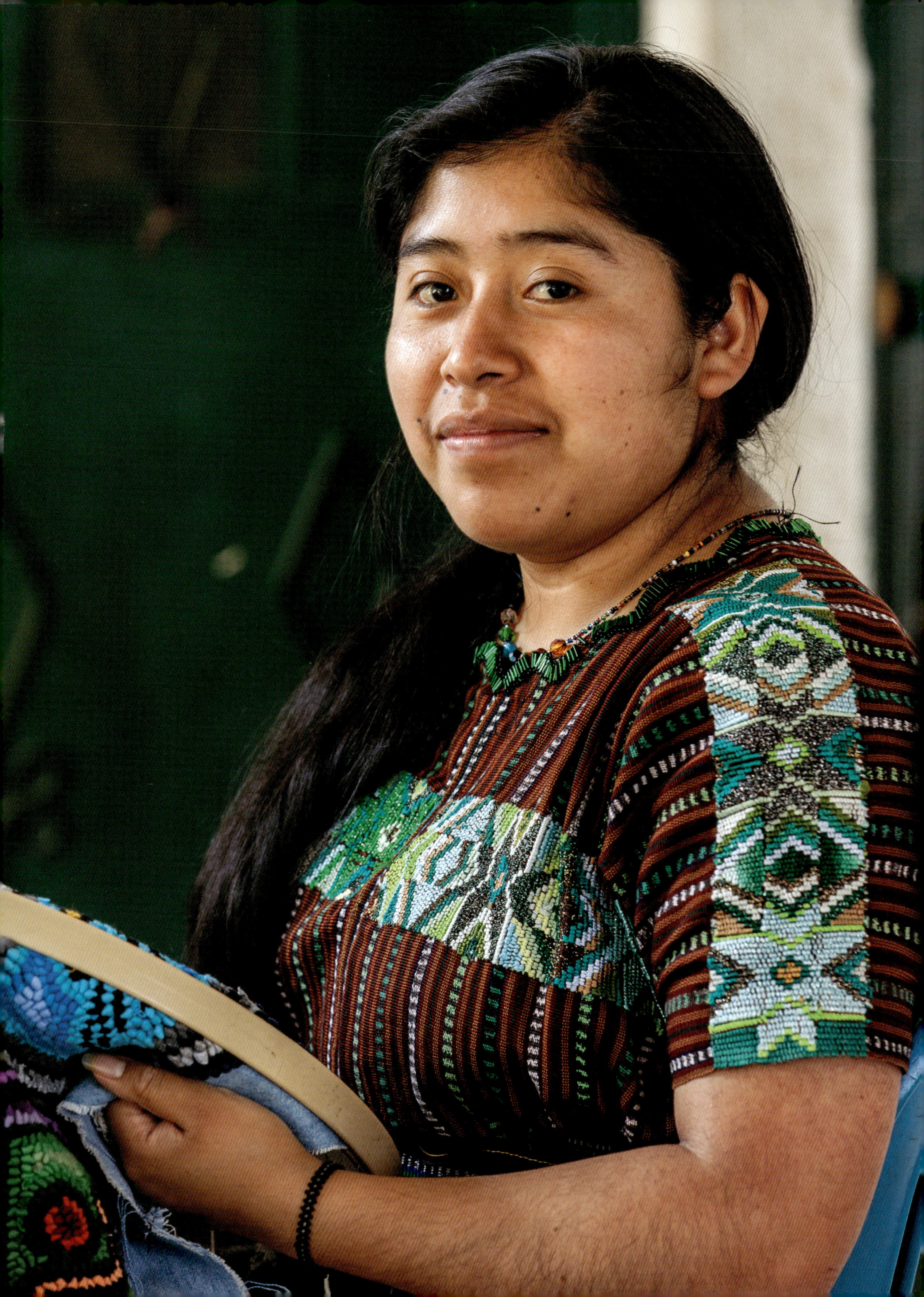

"If you keep working at your art, you can achieve anything"
» Irma Raquel Churunel Aju, 25, Chuacruz

Irma lives in a hilly, picturesque farming community on the outskirts of Solola. She lives with her mother, father, and two sisters. Her other siblings, two brothers and a sister, live in La Capital, where they work and attend school. She is an active member of her church, where she learned to sing. When she is not at church, she awakes each morning eager to work on her rugs, explaining, "Rug making is satisfying work."

Irma and her sisters learned weaving from their mother and each of them weave their own huipils. Her mother still weaves huipils for income, but Irma and her sisters now hook rugs, too. "I used to make money at beadwork, weaving huipils, and sometimes embroidering corte. When I saw Micaela learn the technique from Yolanda and Glendy, I knew I wanted to learn. It wasn't just that I could earn more money making hooked rugs, I wanted the challenge. It's not easy, and to become good at the craft requires a lot of patience."

Irma is one of Multicolores's newest members. She and her sisters, Micaela and Yolanda, achieved the enviable accomplishment of developing their own recognizable style. She attributes this accomplishment to workshops she has taken at Multicolores and to continually improving her skills.

In doing this work, I have learned many things—how to design rugs, how to combine colors, even how to draw. I didn't know I had that skill, and now when Reyna calls me an artist, well, maybe I earned the title because of my new abilities. When I hear Reyna call me an artist, I feel good. It gives me a good feeling inside because I have worked hard, and I put a lot of myself into my designs. I can call myself an artist now with all humbleness. I have a very supportive family, and we all encourage one another. When I get home from a workshop at Multicolores, I share the information with my sisters. We notice how the new skills we learn help our other textile work, too, like combining colors with our beadwork.

Income earned from rug making helps her younger sister and brother attend school in La Capital. As one of Multicolores's top income earners, she is able to offer significant help to her siblings. Micaela and Yolanda, who also live at home, have health issues and use their rug money to buy medicine. The family understands that without Irma's help, her brother and sister would have a difficult time affording their education. Irma views helping them as an investment, saying, "It is their turn now. When they are finished with their schooling, I hope they will help me go to school."

When asked about her goals, Irma says she hopes to continually evolve as an artist. "Each rug that Multicolores sells is unique. It's like the artist has put a bit of herself into the rug. We can't be copied because it comes from inside of us. I think that is the secret of our success. As an artist, I believe I can achieve anything. Sometimes there will be difficulties but it doesn't matter how many disappointments you have had. If you keep working at your art, you can achieve anything."

Reyna, hand-in-hand with Cheryl, created the new leadership program for the Multicolores artists.

Steps toward the Future: Goals for 2017–2018

Savings Program

Another key to improving one's quality of life is learning how to save money, regardless of income. The team envisioned a plan to involve and educate the entire family regarding the benefits of saving money. The class will be broken down into small, achievable goals conducted over three, six, and twelve months. The objective is to help the artists eventually open savings accounts, improve their financial literacy, and establish profitable, lifelong monetary habits.

Health

The team envisions ongoing hand-health workshops with Ann Fox and nutrition classes with another nurse and friend of the project, Pam Marble. Multicolores also aspires to partner with Women's International Network for Guatemala Solutions (WINGS), a Guatemalan-based NGO that offers family planning to its members. In addition, responding to complaints about headaches, likely a result of eye strain, the organization will partner with *Soluciones Comunitarias* (Community Solutions) to conduct eye examinations. If prescription eyeglasses are recommended, Multicolores will pay half the cost; the artist will pay the other half. As with the furniture program, the artists may deduct the payment from rug money over time.

The team noted that four of the ten Planificación de Vida workshop participants requested psychological counseling. In response to their request and addressing what Reyna referred to as "their inside wounds," counseling will be available to those selected for the Leadership Program.

The Three-Year Leadership Program
» Multicolores Office, Panajachel, Guatemala, 2017 and Beyond

The objective of the Planificación de Vida workshop had been fulfilled, and the team learned more about the lives of the Multicolores membership. Listening to the women's stories and responding with effective programming helped Reyna articulate a thought long residing in the back of her mind. Simply put, she wanted to mentor the women of Multicolores in the way she had been mentored. Speaking about her long-ago decision to apply for the store manager job at OB, where she met and befriended Cheryl, Jody, and me, she explains: *I wanted that job to learn how to run a business. I envisioned that owning a business was in my near future. But through working on this project with all of you, I learned things about myself I hadn't realized. You all believed in me, you saw potential in me I didn't know was there, and that helped me believe in myself and envision new possibilities. I grew into the person I am today, helping to run a nonprofit and creating opportunities for Maya women because you all believed in me. I now want the same opportunities for the women of Multicolores. I want to help them reach their potential.*

To help the women of Multicolores reach their potential, the team designed a Leadership Program. The program will take place over the next three years. As in the rug-hooking teacher training project, methodologies will be creative and expert facilitators will lead the training when necessary.

Nine artists from five communities were invited to participate in the program. Reyna and Cheryl identified these women according to their skills, motivation,

Colors of the Future

and leadership abilities. The team believes this group of nine will, over the course of three years, learn to strengthen their natural leadership abilities and become agents of change in their homes, rug-hooking groups, and communities. The approach will be holistic, recognizing that to be a good leader you have to be self-aware along with having good organizational and technical skills. The leaders will become ambassadors, able to confidently represent Multicolores at national and international markets and events. Having learned English and public speaking skills, the leaders will be able to speak about Multicolores's vision and mission, drawing upon their own personal experiences.

Proposed leadership workshops:
- Basic gender sensitivity training
- Finding my voice: communication, English, and public speaking
- Building consensus through negotiation and conflict resolution
- Motivating a team
- Taking care of our minds and our bodies (yoga, meditation, benefits of good nutrition, rest)
- Acquiring technical knowledge by overseeing production and delivery processes including quality control

Organizational efficiencies may be gained by transferring these responsibilities to the groups, as the leaders learn conflict resolution skills and enjoy more autonomy in their group's oversight. Reyna's purpose-filled vision, Cheryl's tireless dedication and pragmatism, and Aura's self-motivation and compassion are shaping Multicolores's future. The determined team realizes that an effective presence of Maya women in the social, economic, and political structures in Guatemala is rooted in the socioeconomic conditions of women. They understand

Leandra Robles receives input on her rug from a compañera in her Totonicapán rug-hooking group. BELOW: Rug hooked by Irma de Leon.

Colors of the Future 139

Sisters-in-law Eva and Nicolasa enjoying time with other members of the Patanatic hooking group who meet twice a month at Glendy's home to work together and offer support and encouragement. BELOW: Juana Calel's daughter Adriana appreciates the benefits of her mother's rug-hooking income.

that there is a deeply embedded belief that the realm of decision-making belongs to men. In order to increase democratic participation, leaders within Multicolores's artisan groups must be identified, trained in topics related to leadership and women's rights, and placed in positions of responsibility within the organization. Positive and well-trained group leaders have tremendous potential to affect the democracy, integrity, and success of communities and groups.

Within the rural communities where we work there is little or no inclusion of women in decision-making processes. We anticipate that the women who take part in the upcoming three-year leadership training will expand their understanding of gender equality.

We feel comfortable in our prediction because we witnessed the changes that occurred when these women accessed the rug-hooking opportunity, mastered a new skill, and began to view themselves as artists capable of success in the marketplace. The change in their self-perception triggered a change in their family dynamics.

Young girls and boys expanded their views of their mothers to include descriptions like "artist" and "entrepreneur." Louisa explains it like this: "My children are happy to see me participate in this work. They see that I am motivated and content with my life because I have become a rug-hooking artist. They see that I am helping with some of the household bills, and I feel good to know they are aware of my contributions. We have a new tradition they really like, and that is when I come home from making a delivery to the office, I stop to buy drinking chocolate and sweet bread. When I get home, we share this treat together; it's a way of celebrating my hard work, and I like to involve them in my success."

As the artists contributed finances to help sustain their households, husbands began to value and support their wives' endeavors, altering their behavior to accommodate the work their wives performed. Teaching leadership skills and "tools for life," we expect the artists to become more confident, reach for their potential, and claim influential roles within their groups and their communities.

Conclusion

María Ignacia's day began at 4 a.m. Securing the knot on her tzute containing everything she would need for her two days away from home, she cast a glance around the room a final time. She'd prepared her family's morning meal, and the pan now rested on the stove waiting to be reheated when her family awoke. Satisfied that her house was in order, she stepped across the threshold into the predawn light. Hoisting the tzute on top of her head and adjusting the balance of the heavy bundle, she began her long walk to the highway.

María Ignacia was off to Panajachel, a four-hour journey by foot and by bus. It was too early in the day for a microbus to pass by and offer a ride, so she budgeted time to include the forty-minute walk to the highway. At the highway, she would await a *camioneta* (bus) and three transfers later, she would arrive at the Multicolores office.

She anticipated this journey with pleasure because she was invited to participate in another workshop at Multicolores. The name of this workshop was called Planificación de Vida. She wasn't sure what that meant, but running the words through her mind, she liked the hopeful sound of it. She loved attending Multicolores's workshops, saying, "I like learning new things; it's satisfying to know I'm capable of doing the work." She wondered if her rug-hooking teacher and friend, Yolanda, would participate, too. Four years ago, in 2013, when Yolanda came to her village as Multicolores's roving rug-hooking ambassador, María Ignacia was invited to join the class. At first, she didn't think she could do the work, but through patience, perseverance, and Yolanda's encouragement, she mastered the technique and was soon designing her own rugs. María Ignacia is quick to convey her gratitude not only for Yolanda's initial workshops but for Reyna, too, who offered constructive criticism along the way. "I always want to hear how I can improve my quality, my designs, and my colors. Reyna had a lot of patience with me; without her help, I couldn't succeed."

When asked what she likes best about Multicolores, María Ignacia says "I look forward to coming to the office because it feels like visiting family. I had a difficult childhood; my father neglected my siblings and me. My father died, and that is when my mother started drinking a lot. Now my siblings think what I am doing with my life is wrong. They think I should stay home and take care of my husband and my children. But I know in my heart what I have accomplished with rug hooking, and I know the ongoing training I do with Multicolores is the best thing for my family. I have stopped caring what my siblings think. They can live their own lives."

During her long commute to the Multicolores office, María Ignacia's thoughts drift back to previous workshops.

She remembers the 2016 class on color taught by Keith Recker, a man from Los Estados Unidos. His class made her think about things she'd never considered, things like naming all the colors. She recalls being surprised to learn that a color she thought of as "leaf green" was called "*aguacate*" (avocado) by her compañeras. But in his workshop, they agreed upon names to give all the colors and by the end of his workshop, everyone left with the same set of color swatches cut from their paca.

Returning home from Keith's workshop, she taped the color swatches to a wall in the room where she hooks. Her swatches are organized according to color families, in the same manner Keith taught. When her group comes to her house to hook, they sometimes discuss a member's rug, a rug that may need reworking because of a problem with colors. They can now point to the swatches pinned to her wall and offer specific suggestions, knowing everyone has the same color in mind.

A year later, in early 2017, María Ignacia was selected to participate in a workshop conducted by Mary Flanagan from Los Estados Unidos. Mary, a maker and designer, offered the first in a series of workshops to create new products from the rug-hooking technique. Speaking about the opportunity to participate in another workshop, María Ignacia acknowledges the trust the organization places in her. She feels eager to rise to their expectations saying, "They believe in me and that is a good feeling. And I really like learning to make something new. It's not just rugs anymore; we now have more options for things to make."

Sitting on the crowded camioneta, María Ignacia's thoughts return to the day stretching before her. She is proud to have earned the respect of Multicolores's staff and she looks forward to seeing them again. She knows the organization holds her in regard, a fact that helped her overcome a recent disappointment.

In 2017, she was selected to represent her compañeras at the International Folk Art Market. She recalls the excitement of getting a passport; she knows only one other person in her community—including her family—who owns a passport (Carmen, who represented the rug hookers at the IFAM in 2015). She describes the excitement of traveling to the U.S. embassy in Guatemala City, where she spent the night prior to her interview. However, during her visa interview, the official asked only three questions. (1) What is your husband's job? ("He works at a gas station.") (2) How many children do you have? ("Two.") (3) Why are you going to the United States? ("To represent my compañeras at the International Folk Art Market in Santa Fe, New Mexico.") The official stamped her application "Denied" and said, "Get out, this interview is over." Poised and thinking on her feet, María Ignacia politely asked the official to "please read my letter of invitation from the IFAM." But the woman refused, saying, "I don't have to. It's not mandatory."

In recalling the experience, María Ignacia said, "I went into that interview knowing I had the support of Multicolores. The woman at the embassy couldn't take that away from me. I still have Multicolores's support, and that means more to me than a visa. Realizing this gift I had from Multicolores, my disappointment was gone."

Reflecting on her experiences with Multicolores, she wishes others in her community could have the same opportunity. She speculates that if others could access the opportunities she has enjoyed, her village would be a happier place. "I know this because, through the opportunities I have enjoyed, not just the income but working with an organization that cares about me, I have become a more content person. I learn tools to not only help me with my art but also with my life."

142 Colors of the Future

Notes

Preface

Page vii. Indrasen Vencatachellum, "Introduction: Valuing Folk Art in the 21st Century," in *The Work of Art* (Santa Fe, NM: AFAA Media, 2010) 11–13.2.

Page ix. Robert Chambers, *Whose Reality Counts? Putting the First Last* (London: Intermediate Technology Publications, 1997).

PART I

Page 3. Minneapolis Trunk Shows were hosted by Stephanie Odegard of Odegard Carpets and included the following interior design firms: Carol Belz and Associates; Wendy Coggins; Barnhouse Office Interior Design; Gunkelmans Interior Design; Shadowfalls Design; Gay Parker; and Morine Design. The Denver Trunk Show was hosted by Marcia Kahn of The Rug Source in Denver and included the following interior design firms: Associates III; Company KD; Jordan Design Studio; In-Site Design Group, Inc.; Mullen Design; Ronnberg Associates, Inc.

Page 3. For over two decades, Farmer to Farmer has worked to support peace and cross-cultural understanding. Today, the organization helps small coffee farmers through a yearly commitment to import 23,000 pounds of green coffee beans. This commitment assures the farmers an annual income. In addition, Farmer to Farmer offers scholarships to some of the farmers' children.

Page 6. Most North American rug hookers hook with strips of wool cloth, both new and recycled. However, wool fabric is a valuable recycled commodity and is culled long before it reaches Guatemala.

Page 73. In 2016, Multicolores initiated a project to train embroiderers. The objectives and training curriculum were based on the rug-hooking project and began in June 2016. As this book goes to press, the training is ongoing.

PART II

Page 87. The International Folk Art Market is an annual two-and-a-half-day juried sales event and festival. It takes place in July on Museum Hill in Santa Fe, New Mexico, home to the International Folk Art Museum. Participation is open to folk artists living in countries around the globe except the United States. In 2015, it was voted #1 Art Festival by *USA Today's* readers. In 2016, over 634 applicants from 83 countries applied for approximately 160 slots offered for the 2017 Market.

PART III

Page 110. The artisan sector is the second-largest employer in the developing world after agriculture, worth over $32 billion every year. Hundreds of thousands of people across the globe, particularly women, participate in the artisan sector. Artisan activity creates jobs, increases local incomes, and preserves ancient cultural traditions that in many places are at risk of being lost.
http://www.allianceforartisanenterprise.org/about/

Page 124. Using data collected from 41 rug hookers, we learned that the average annual household income, from all sources, is $4,073. The average annual cost for household expenses (food, rent, transport, medicine, education, electricity, wood, gas, potable water, cable, loan) is $3,691 leaving a balance of $382. Given the competition for other needs, the decision to buy the furniture may be interpreted to mean the women placed a high value on the opportunity to improve their working conditions. In 2016, the three highest incomes earned from rug hooking were $2,805, $2,580, and $1,947. In some cases, the women contribute more than half of the household's yearly income.

Page 132. Minimum wage summaries as reported by the Ministry of Work:
http://www.mintrabajo.gob.gt/index.php/salariominimo.html

Page 138. http://www.solucionescomunitarias.com/guatemala

Photography Credits

All photography by Joe Coca except for the following:

Cheryl Walsh Bellville: page 48

Michael Benanav: page 33

Nikki Brand: page 12

Phyllis Bretholtz: pages 10, 45, 46, 47

Lorna Call: pages 79 (bottom), 88, and 89

Rachel Green: pages 17, 24, 73 (top), 96 and 138

Multicolores staff: pages 4, 5, 11, 13, 18-19, 21, 22 (bottom), 23, 25, 29, 36, 41, 42, 43, 52, 54-55, 56 (bottom), 58, 60-61, 65, 67, 69, 75-77, 90-91, 94, 105, 107 (bottom), 108 (bottom), 109, 110 (top), 113 (bottom), 115, 116 (bottom), 117 (bottom), 119 (bottom), 1121 (bottom), 124, 125 (top), 127–128, 129 (bottom), 130-131, 133 (bottom), 135 (bottom)

Van Hart/Shutterstock: page 40

Alliance Organizations

Alliance Organizations Supporting Women, Art, and Innovation

Anderson Center www.andersoncenter.org

Alliance for Artisan Enterprise www.artisanalliance.org

Avenir Museum www.avenir.colostate.edu

ClothRoads www.clothroads.com

Cultural Cloth www.culturalcloth.com

Farmer to Farmer www.farmer-to-farmer.org

Friendship Bridge www.friendshipbridge.org

International Folk Art Alliance/International Folk Art Market
www.folkartmarket.org

Maya Educational Foundation www.mayaedufound.org

Maya Traditions Foundation www.mayatraditions.org

Mayan Hands www.mayanhands.org

Mil Milagros/A Thousand Miracles www.milmilagros.org

Museo Ixchel de Traje Indigena/Ixchel Museum of Indigenous Dress
www.museoixchel.org

Multicolores Guatemala www.multicolores.org

Oxlajuj B'atz' (OB) www.oxlajujbatz.wordpress.com

Sharing the Dream www.sharingthedream.org

Soluciones Comunitarias/Community Solutions
www.solucionescomunitarias.com

Textile Center, Minneapolis, Minnesota www.textilecentermn.org

Textile Museum of Canada www.textilemuseum.ca

Weave A Real Peace (WARP) www.weavearealpeace.org

Women's International Network for Guatemala Solutions (WINGS)
www.wingsguate.org

Index

A
AGEXPORT 67

Alfombras 20

Anderson Arts Center 20, 21, 23, 24, 25, 26, 88, 105

Antigua 39–40

Alliance for Artisan Enterprise 110, 146

Avenir Museum 105, 146

B
Balzer, JoAnn and Bob 95

Barriletes (kites) 88

C
Calel, Juana **80, 114–117**; daughter 140

Calgua, Yessika 11, 25, **62, 84, 104**, 105

Calgua, Yolanda vii, 9–11, **14**, 21, 24-25, 37, 41, 42–43, 45, 49, 57, **58**, 61, 62, 63, **64–67**, 72, 78, 84, 87–88, **89, 104, 105**, 111, 141

Calgua, Zoila x, 15, 37, 44, **45, 47**, 54, 60, 69, 70, 78, 87, 88, **89**, 105

Can, Aura Perez **122**, 123–125, 139

Chandler, Deborah 1, 4, 6, 11

Chichicastenango 3, 8, 9, 14, 65

Chirijquiac 29, 61, 97, 132; Chirijquiac rug-hooking group **98–99**

Chuacruz 133, 135; Chuacruz rug-hooking group **100–101**

Churunel, Irma **100, 134–137**

Churunel, Micaela 59, 93, **95, 100, 101**, 135, 137

Civil war, Guatemala 8

Conway-Daly, Cheryl ix, 71–72, **73**, 87, 89–90, 92, 92–95, **96**, 97, 10, 103, 105, **110**, 112–113, 122–124, 132, 138–139

Cua, Carmen 71

Cultural Cloth 26, 61, 89, 97, 146

D
de Leon, Irma 139

Design principles 41–44, 56, 65, 78

E
Easter, Jennifer 33

F
Farmer to Farmer 3, 9, 144, 146

Flanagan, Mary 142

Fox, Ann 110

Friendship Bridge 3, 65, 146

Furniture project 123–124

G
Gonzales, Javier 95

Guatemala City 37–39, 97, 142

H
Huipils 1, 12, 20, **34**, 39, 41, 42, 55, 111, 135

I
Iglesia La Merced **40**

International Folk Art Market (IFAM) vii, 1, 41, 77, 87, 88, 90–97, 103, 142, 146

Itzep, Tomasa **98, 110**

Ixcaco 41

J
Joj, Walter Amilcar **130**, 131

K
Kirschenman, Ramona 4, 6, 10, 24, 20, 24, 25, 26, 71–72

Knoke, Barbara 39

L
Lake Atitlán 3, 4, 32, 37, 39, 51, 108

Leadership Program 138–140

Littrell, Mary vii–x

M

Maldonado, Carmen 1, 9, 11, 12–13, 21, 22, 27, **28–31**, 36, **41**, 42, 44–45, **46, 49, 56**, 58, **69**, 70, 78–79, 93, **94**, 95, **96–97, 98–99**

Maya Traditions Foundation 4, 6, 10, 33, 45, 57, 65, 146

Mayan Hands 1, 4, 11, 146

Mendoza, Glendy **50–53**, 34, 36, 37, 42–43, 47, **54**, 58, 72, 78–79, **80**, 93–95, 107, 109, 115–117, **125**

Mil Milagros/A Thousand Miracles 72, 146

Morales, Bartola 44, **80, 106–109**

Multicolores, organization formed 72–73

Museo Ixchel de Traje Indigena/Ixchel Museum of Indigenous Dress 37, 39, 146

N

Nauhales 130–131

Nesselhuf, Diane 4

O

Oxlajuj B'atz' (OB) 4, 6, 13, 14, 20, 22, 26, 27, 45, 54, 55, 71, 72

P

Paca 5, 6, 10, 44, 45, 58–59, 97, 104, 107, 111, 117, 123, 124, 132

Pacay, Nicolasa **80**, **113**, **124**, 125, **140**

Pacheco, Rosmery 10, 37, 39, 46, 59, **68**, 69, 72, **74–77**, 79, **82, 92**, 94

Panajachel 1, 2, 5, 14, 32, 37, 38, 88, 93, 122, 141

Patanatic 51, 11, 115; Patanatic rug-hooking group **80–81**

Planificación de Vida (Life Plan) 124–125

Pretzantzin, Reyna ix, 32, **33**, 34–36, 40–41, 45–47, 49, 54–55, **58**, 59–60, 61, 72, 78–79, 87, 90–93, **94, 96**, 103, 105, **110**, 113, 123, 125, 131–133, 138–139

Q

Quiejel 24, 65, 104; Quiejel rug-hooking group **84–85**

R

Recker, Keith 131, 141

Reiche, Olga 41

Rixquiacche, Pascuala 113

Rug-hooking tours ix, 19, 46, 47, 53, 92, 117

S

Sacalxot, María **12**, 23, 34, 46, 59, **72**, 97, **98–99**, 110

Salcajá 4

San Jorge La Laguna 107–108

Semana Santa 20

Sharing the Dream 4, 146

Slocum, Jody ix, 3–9, 14, 21–22, **24**, 26, 41, 55, 69–70, 72, 89, 90, 92, 94–95, 97

Sololá 3, 135

Soluciones Comunitarias/Community Solutions 135, 145, 146

T

Tamayac, Maria Estela Az 37, 133

Teacher Training 32–49, 54–63, 68–70

Teacher Training Graduation 71–72

Textile Center, Minneapolis, Minnesota 105, 109, 146

Textile Museum of Canada 22, 105, 146

Tipica 38

Todos Santos (All Saints Festival) 88

Totonicapán 17, 27, 35, 71, 75, 92; Totonicapán rug-hooking group **82–83**, 128

Traje vii, 3, 13, 14, 34, 38, 42–43

Tzunun, Hilda **12, 56, 82**, 112, **126–129**

Tzunun, Ramona 15, **16–19**, 21, 34, **41**, 57, 59

Tzutes 1, **48**

U

University of Rafael Landivar 32

V

Ventura, Tomasa **26, 84, 85**

Vicente, María Ignacia 67, **98**, **110**, 111, **118–121**, 141–142

W

Wise, Mary Anne **24**, **35, 36, 54, 55, 69**

Women's International Network for Guatemala Solutions (WINGS) 138, 146